Celebrate Kids

More Great Ideas
for
Stay-at-Home Moms

Angie Peters

SAINT LOUIS

For Nick, Lindsey, and Erin

Scripture quotations are taken from the HOLY BIBLE, NEW INTERNATIONAL VERSION®. NIV®. Copyright © 1973, 1978, 1984 by International Bible Society. Used by permission of Zondervan Publishing House. All rights reserved.

Copyright © 2000 Concordia Publishing House
3558 S. Jefferson Avenue
St. Louis, MO 63118-3968
Manufactured in the United States of America

—————————— Library of Congress Cataloging-in-Publication Data ——————————

Peters, Angie. 1964-
  Celebrate kids! : more great ideas for stay-at-home moms / Angie Peters.
    p.   cm.
  ISBN 0-570-05229-7
  1. Mothers. 2. Motherhood. 3. Child rearing. 4. Parent and child.
HQ759.P46873 2000
306.874'3–dc21   99-055105

1 2 3 4 5 6 7 8 9 10   09 08 07 06 05 04 03 02 01 00

Acknowledgments

Two important dates——the June birth of my daughter, Erin Leah, and the April completion of our home renovations—sandwiched my May deadline for this manuscript. Loving thanks to everyone who cheered me over the hurdles. Terry, thanks for saying, "You can do it" more times than I can count. Tonya, you're the best girlfriend a girl could have whether you're five minutes or five hours away. Thanks for keeping my battery charged when my energy and optimism ran low, and for keeping my kids when I needed to write. Mom and Dad, thank you for a lifetime supply of love and support. Kurt, thanks for so much, and especially for retrieving that lost file. *You're always my hero.*

I'm also grateful to all the moms who generously shared their experiences and insights with me for this book: Gina Cash, whose friendship I treasure and who makes being a school mom even more fun; the moms from the Spring Creek MOPS group and the WAHM list members who responded to my survey questions; and Andrea Batchelor, Bonnie Skinner, Sharon Hoffman, and Holly Schurter, busy moms who graciously agreed to spare the time to be interviewed.

Contents

Preface

The morning I got the go-ahead from my editor at Concordia to write this book, I had just dusted the top of our oak entertainment center with spray starch.

A sign surely. That I can't always be counted on to keep my cans of cleaning products straight made me think that while I may have been on the ball enough to write my first book five years ago when I had a twenty-something-year-old brain, my literary prospects as a thirtyish mother-of-two-with-another-on-the-way might be dim. I had keyed in *Celebrate Home* in the warm, "those-were-the-days" days of first steps and fairy tales; of pacifiers and fleece footed pjs; of *Goodnight, Moon* and Tinkertoys. I could tuck my two under-fours in at 7:30 P.M. and then spend three or four delicious evening hours a week channeling an abundant supply of creative energy into crafting the book that was my love letter to stay-at-home moms everywhere.

But now, my first grader and third grader some-times tuck *me* in at 7:30 P.M., a lethargic, first-trimester mom, battle weary from the day's relentless schedule which seems at times to run me rather than me it. Have I *thought* too much? That last episode of having to strategize a way to get Nick to Boy Scouts and to round up and transport a meal to the home of a precious friend, Gina, whose son's appendix had just been removed on a day that my couch was in the kitchen because I had to shampoo the carpet after an untimely but thorough flea infestation (what would be a *timely* one?)—did successfully choreographing that crazy dance use up the only viable brain cells I had left? How on earth would I be able to encourage, motivate, inspire others in their journey as full-time moms when the map of my own route is so wrinkled and has Mountain Berry flavored Kool-Aid stains on it?

But as I tried to figure out what effect hairspray might have on the sticky layer of starch coating the top of my entertainment center, I remembered one key element to what I do when I write. I never propose to have all the answers. I don't pretend to live a life even remotely worthy of imitation. I don't say, "do as I do" or even "do as I say." I simply revert to my pre-kids role as a journalist. A reporter. Only now, instead of handling business news, motherhood's my beat. More specifically, stay-at-home motherhood, in all its varied and wonderful definitions.

Relieved of the obligation to know all the answers, I decided to tackle the book after all. I would just report the whos-whats-wheres-whens-whys-and-hows that the real experts—other moms—have to offer about some of the subjects moms of 5-to-12-year-olds care about most. I would ask them about the issues that challenge us every day—from the formal education of our kids to getting (and staying) organized. And just in case you're interested, one of the first interview questions I planned to ask once I began setting up interviews was

"How do you remove a flaky white layer of spray starch from the top of an entertainment center?"

Introduction

Stay-at-Home Moms Staying at Home

"Free at last, free at last!" many tired moms feel like shouting as the bright yellow school bus pulls away from the curb to tote their last-born to the first day of kindergarten.

This day, after all, marks the end of an era for lots of women who exited the mommy track to be at home full-time only until their children reached school age. They marched into stay-at-home motherhood knowing their mission on the home front would be short-term; now they are ready to unearth the briefcase from the back of the closet, refill their Day-Timers, and rejoin the ranks of the paid full-time workforce.

Statistics show these moms are in the majority: Nearly 70 percent of married couples with school-age children (between the ages of 6 and 17) were both employed in 1997, and that number continues to grow each year. One estimate indicates that as many as 5 million American latch-key kids go home to empty houses after school each day because both parents work during those hours.

But some moms opt to remain home for a few more years, some even indefinitely, either by staying out of the paid workforce altogether or by seeking part-time, flex-time, or work-at-home arrangements.

Catie, mother of two, says she decided to remain at home after her children started school because

> **I remember when I was in the sixth grade. I would come home to an empty house after school. Every day I would call my mom at work just to let her know I arrived safe. It didn't seem necessary for me back then, but I did it because it was important to my mom. I didn't understand why back then, but I do now. I couldn't imagine having my kids come home to an empty house now. I have only been at home for one year since leaving my job. It has been the best thing I ever did for my family.**

—Amanda, mother of four

she wants simply to *be there* for her kids. "Being around whenever my kids need me, not when my job allows," she says, "is a priceless benefit no company can offer!"

The decision, she says, was not one she had expected to make.

"When my first was born, I almost immediately calculated out how many years I would have to wait to return to the work force," she says. "I repeated the same calculations when my second arrived two years later." But "my oldest started preschool last year, and I'm happy to say that I have no intention of returning to an office outside of my home! Ever!"

For moms like Gina, the desire to remain at home for son Bradley and daughter Melody through their school-age years hasn't come as a surprise. She never for a moment planned to reenter the workforce during that time because she has always recognized that her children "have even greater needs for me when they are in school. I want to be able to be involved in their school and other activities," she says. "I don't think I could juggle it all and work outside the home too."

Many other moms remain in the stay-at-home category after the kids reach school age because of their strong convictions to homeschool. In fact, according to the Home School Legal Defense Association, 87.5 percent of moms (and 0.5 percent of dads) who homeschool opt to stay home full-time in order to teach and raise their children.

Although continuing to forgo career for kids may not be the right choice—or even an option—for everyone, moms who make that decision generally do so because they believe that stay-at-home motherhood is the best forum for guiding their kids through the school-age years. This book is written with these moms (including me!) in mind. *Celebrate Kids* will, I pray, help us keep the pace—and the peace—during these pivotal and oh-so-busy grade-school years by inspiring us to commit to creating godly homes; by educating us about school issues; by urging us to keep a constant physical as well as eternal eye on our kids; by giving us much-needed ideas when we're too tired to come up with them on our own; and by encouraging us to be confident, creative, consistent, and caring as we shepherd our flocks through these days. This book will remind us that, armed with a continued focus on God and His grace, and a day-by-day, minute-by-minute dependence on His strength, protection, and guidance, we won't merely survive; we can truly celebrate these crazy but crucial years of being our kids' moms.

> " I like my mom being at home... 'acause I like to play dolls and snuggle and watch TV and I love my brother and my dad and my mom and I love my cat and my dog. "
> —Melody, age 3

One Mom's Story

"Staying home is more stress, more work, and more rewarding than work ever was."
—Andrea Batchelor

When Andrea Batchelor left her job as a news anchor for the NBC affiliate in Orlando in November 1996 to stay home with her three sons, she left behind a situation which many would describe as "having it all."

"I had, all the way around, as ideal a situation as you could get," she says. "First of all, I had part-time hours in a very high-paying career—a six-figure income for just a few hours a day. I had a baby-sitter who was outstanding. She was just wonderful, a committed Christian with great values and a real love for the boys. She took care of everything around the house. There wasn't ever a worry that she wouldn't handle a situation the right way. So it was all very good."

So ... what's wrong with *that* picture?

"What was not right was that I was not having enough time with my children."

When the kids—Richard, 11, David, 8½, and Matthew, 5—reached school age, Andrea explains, her position as 6:00 news anchor called her to be away from home precisely when her sons were at home.

"First of all, the baby-sitter would go and pick them up from school and she would make their dinner and they would do their homework. By the time I got home, between 6:30 and 7:00, they were tired. They had already been through everything. I'd say, 'How was your day?' They'd say, 'Fine.' We just weren't getting enough time together."

Changing careers from broadcasting to full-time mom hadn't been a part of Andrea's original plans. "I had a working mom and I just didn't see myself as a stay-at-home mom until I had the kids," she says. "It was a slow turnaround. It wasn't an overnight thing. It just finally became apparent that that's what I wanted to do and needed to do."

On her last day at work, she didn't have the doubts or misgivings that some moms experience when confronted with the finality of their dramatic decision. "That day I just had this resolve and a real peace about what I was doing," she says. "When you do the right thing and you know you're doing what God wants you to do, it's very peaceful."

Since then, Andrea says she hasn't had any of the second thoughts some colleagues had predicted. "I had some who thought I would regret it and miss it," she says, "but I just didn't. There has not been a day or an hour of the day where I haven't been absolutely 100 percent sure that what I did was the right thing. I'm really pleased that I did it."

Once home, Andrea says she immediately saw the benefits of her job change. "... the second night [after I quit], I asked my husband, 'Do you notice a difference in the kids, in the family dynamics?' He said, 'Yes.' I said, 'Do you notice a calm?' He said, 'Yes.' ... It was kind of like God telling me, 'You did the right thing.' "

Andrea says she thinks staying home with her kids will continue to be "the right thing" for the Batchelor family "until the kids are grown."

"The older they get," she believes, "the more important it is to be around. My mother always said that. In some ways almost anybody can hug a baby but you've got to be there when they're older. I've been able to do field trips, I've been able to be the room mother and to volunteer in the lunchroom ... to do all those things. Being there makes a big difference ... they see themselves as a priority."

part I

Kids under Construction:

The Safety Zone of Home

chapter 1

Home Is Where a Kid's Start Is

"Pour out your heart like water in the presence of the Lord. Lift up your hands to Him for the lives of your children."—*Lamentations 2:19*

When the Creator God organized what we know as the world, He arranged the human part of His creation into families. Beginning with Adam and Eve, He has shown us throughout history that, for better or worse, families are the perfect greenhouses in which to plant and nurture each tender growing life. It's no accident that God saw fit to place even His only Son within the loving arms of a family.

This basic unit of humankind has endured throughout the ages. Issues affecting family and home continue to ignite powerful passions that cross geographical, cultural, religious, and economic borders worldwide. Most of us wouldn't have swerved off the career track to be stay-at-home moms if we didn't feel so strongly about the crucial nature of home and family in raising our kids. We may have these intense feelings about our family life because we were raised in homes and families with qualities that we'd like to pass on to our kids. On the other hand, we may do so because we *weren't* raised in ideal situations and we'd like to give our kids what we never had. Regardless of the psychology that drives our parenting ambitions, we should, in the hubbub of everyday life, remember to stay focused on the foundations of a solid home.

Love and Marriage

"Has not the LORD made them one?"
Malachi 2:15

"... and when youth has passed, may they be found then, as now, still hand in hand, still thanking God for each other. May they serve You happily, and faithfully, until one shall lay the other into the arms of God."

Thirteen Christmases, three pregnancies, four moves, eight vehicles, five baseball seasons, two dance recitals, 12 class projects, and 3,978 loads of laundry have tumbled through our lives since the pastor voiced that sweet wedding prayer over our bowed heads as we clutched each other's hands in a church full of friends and family one rainy May Saturday night.

At the time, Rev. Logue probably had no idea what an impact his tender blessing was to have on that 21-year-old girl who was leaving the security and comfort of her mom and dad's home to blaze her own new trail in the unknown wilderness of marriage and homebuilding. Events both mundane and sensational have knocked on our cabin door through the years, threatening, at times, to flip-flop our priorities and minimize the significance of our marriage. I've echoed that prayer so often that it has become permanently etched in my heart. The words remind me that Kurt and I—our relationship, not our circumstances—are the perpetual event that is our marriage. It was just us then: two kids reverently and nervously holding hands before God in that sanctuary full of celebrants. And it's just us now: two parents clinging to the stability and familiarity of each other's hands and the hope we have in Christ as we feel our way through the labyrinth of challenges that guide us through this people-raising adventure.

If we don't do what it takes *now* to keep our marriage sturdy, our love affair alive, we might have to work double-time to repair the damage *then*, when we reach midlife clutching the comfort of each other's hands as we witness the bittersweet milestones—first dates, graduations, marriages—that will carry each of our kids further from our care and closer to independence. So how do we keep our marriage stable, our romance kindled? Is that even possible, given weekly Scout meetings, a 15-pound weight gain, tag-team rampages of chicken pox, incessant interruptive phone calls, unexpected budget-busting expenses? Absolutely! We can start by

Protecting the Partnership

You wouldn't carelessly toss around that antique vase you got from your great-grandma; how much more important is your partnership with your husband? Robert J. Morgan, in his book *Empowered Parenting*, points out that we must guard our marriages (read Malachi 2:15–16) with a protective attitude that becomes a routine and necessary part of life. We should offer an unhesitating *yes* to any activity that enhances, protects, or strengthens our marriage and an uncompromising *no* to any activity that can potentially undermine, damage, or even destroy our relationship.

Investing in the Commitment

What we value in this world is often made evident by the amount of time and money we spend on it. For example, it's obvious that I value reading because I never hesitate to spend either a few minutes or a few dollars on a good book or magazine. As we would spend the time and money to have a treasured wedding gown properly packed, preserved, and stored, we can invest in our marriage by spending time—and yes, even a little money—on our mates. A weekend getaway, a book on marriage enrichment, a baby-sitter for an evening alone, a thoughful gift, a Sunday afternoon walk around the block—all of these can yield generous, marriage-enhancing "interest" on our investment.

Reconnecting Regularly

My husband lays out floor plans for a national depart-ment store chain. He usually works on projects for stores in three or four different cities at one time and, through the years, I've always tried to keep up with which ones he has on his slate. But one night at supper, Kurt mentioned getting approval on a plan for a store that I had no idea he had been working on. We had let our lines of com-munication get so clogged up with the activities of the past few weeks that we hadn't been connecting through any real conversation more meaningful than "What do you want for dinner?" "Will you be home in time to take Lindsey to her soccer prac-tice?" or "I need you to pick up milk and lunchmeat on your way home from work." We hadn't been grabbing any time to reconnect at the end of each evening or even at the end of each week and now we were seeing the results. Although I knew we weren't exactly teetering on the brink of an empty and lifeless marriage, I knew this was a red light calling for quick action. All that we needed to repair this communication breakdown was a date night—either a get-a-sitter-and-go-out-on-the-town night or a let's-grill-steaks-after-the-kids-go-to-bed night. Either option would give us the chance to shift our focus from family, friends, and life in general to each other. Here are some other ways to stay in circuit with our mates in the craziness of a busy family's activities:

≈ Get up 30 minutes earlier than usual each morning to chat over a cup of hot tea or coffee.

≈ Exercise together—walk three times a week, play a set of tennis once a month, fish, camp, etc.

≈ Sit on the front step to watch the kids play together. The kids feel they have your undivided attention but they don't realize you're snatching a real conversation with each other.

≈ Hold hands every chance you get.

≈ Linger at the dinner table after the kids have drifted away to play. The dishes aren't going anywhere.

≈ Don't let the kids derail your stolen moments. A snuggly conversation on the couch on a rainy Sunday afternoon, a Saturday night rerun of the movie you saw on your first date, a spontaneous snack of cookies and milk at the kitchen counter while the kids are getting ready for bed—these are "moments" you don't plan but that can make life with your mate so ... grounded. Kids at times seem designed to destroy these moments with demands of all shapes and sizes. Tell the kids not to interrupt these moments unless they're bleeding or the house is on fire. Some parents will sigh, roll their eyes, and put up the ice cream scoop when little Lacy comes in and says, "I can't find my slippers" or "I'm thirsty." But marriage-minded mates, without taking their eyes off each other, will come up with a loving and gentle way to say, "Not now, we're in the middle of something and we'll take care of your needs after we finish." In a world where marriages are falling apart all around our kids, this message of solidarity will comfort them—whether they realize it or not—by letting them know your marriage is a permanent fixture in their lives.

≈ Spend time with other adults. You don't have to be alone on a date to connect. Sometimes going to a party or on a "double date" with friends can help you enjoy each other just as well. A fun evening with friends makes climbing into the car alone together afterward seem even more intimate.

≈ Try something new together. When my mom mentioned over the phone one day a few years ago that she and Dad had been looking at houseboats, I gasped, "To buy?" My mother and father, who had never camped in my whole life, were going to live for two or three days—maybe even a week or two —at a time, in nothing more than a floating camper? But a couple of months later, my dad, wearing his new captain's hat, was deftly easing a beautiful houseboat out of the dock as my mom, the first mate, adeptly maneuvered the ropes. I looked on, impressed, and imagined what fun and memories they must have made as they learned this new hobby together.

Marking and Making Memories
Remember when you were first dating and first married, how you would save a ticket stub from that special concert to paste into your scrapbook, hang snapshots of your sun-kissed honey at the lake on your bathroom mirror, get misty-eyed when the radio played "your song"? Then the kids came along. Now it's the ticket stubs from the circus you save to stuff into the baby book, snapshots of your baby's first gummy smile that you affix to every vertical surface

of your home, and lullabies that you sang to your 8-year-old when he was a baby that summon the lump in your throat. Your focus has understandably shifted, but take time to travel down those long-ago memory lanes you share with your mate. Look at old snapshots together, reminisce about the "good old days," and make it a point now to mentally file away funny stories and mementos of your current life together. Press that rose he brought you last week because he knew you had a rough day. Tuck away that coffee-stained reminder to pick up the dry cleaning he wrote you last week that had a P.S. that gave you a spring in your step all day: "You're the best. I love you."

Looking Ahead

In these days when we're so busy we can hardly see beyond the next load of laundry, it's important to touch base with our mates from time to time to talk about the big picture. Had you always said you'd like another baby but things have gotten so busy with the kids that you have you just haven't stopped long enough to discuss it? Did you and your mate expect to have made that trip to Europe by the time you reached your mid-30s? Did your husband always say he'd really like to go into business for himself one day? Is it time to consider how to help one of your parents whose health is failing? Have you always wanted to start a home business? If you don't schedule some unstructured time together to allow these conversations to surface, they may not get discussed until the opportunity has passed or until a decision must be made in haste or under pressure. Lots of times these kinds of conversations allow you to revise your plans and dreams as circumstances change. It's nice to get that out in the open too.

Parentlove: Love That Sticks

"DeAr DAD—youR thE BEST you Love mE EvEn wHEn I gEt in TrubEl,"

Lindsey painstakingly wrote in her 6-year-old kidprint across the inside of the folded blue construction paper she was turning into a birthday card for her daddy.

"How's that?" she asked proudly.

As I looked over my daughter's shoulder to praise her handiwork, I inwardly applauded my husband for successfully teaching our little girl one of the most difficult concepts a human can understand: unconditional love.

Maybe one reason God, in His infinite wisdom, subgrouped humans into families is because the love of parents for children, brothers and sisters for brothers and sisters, comes closest to resembling the love He has for us. Where, if not at home, can our children get a glimpse of that "I will never leave you nor forsake you" kind of love illustrated by Jehovah to the Israelites in the wilderness, by God to Jonah in the belly of the fish, by the Lord Jesus to the frightened disciples in a storm-tossed boat, by the resurrected Christ to the entire lost and hurting world?

Family First

Remember the conscience-pricking bumper stickers, popular years ago, that asked fast-tracking tailgaters of the "me generation," "Have you hugged your child today?" A more on-target message stuck to the minivan bumpers of supercharged families today might read: "Where does your family rank on your to-do list?" Does your family's together time keep getting bumped to the bottom of the list by the tyranny of the urgent—ball games, birthday parties, committee meetings?

This hit home in our family when on a recent Friday morning Kurt called as soon as he reached the office.

"I've got an idea," he said. I knew it was going to be a good one by the tone of his voice and because he comes up with some of his best ideas—from vacation destinations to steak dinners—during that morning commute.

"Just wanted to throw it out to you ... let's get up early tomorrow and drive down to Lake Catherine for a hike with the kids. The weather's supposed to be great. Then we'll drive into Hot Springs for lunch and some shopping."

A million-dollar idea that was!

Each of us had been going 90-to-nothing the previous week; Nick had been staying at school until 5:00 or 5:30 each day to work on a class project; Lindsey had been going to friends' houses daily to practice for an upcoming talent show; I had been frantically getting ready to present some workshops at a women's conference; and Kurt had been hammering and sanding into the wee hours each night trying to finish the two rooms we were adding to our house in time for the baby's arrival. That clever spouse of mine had even built something for everyone into our excursion: hiking for him and the kids (now in the "waddling" phase of my pregnancy, a rocky, slippery hike was nothing this mom wanted any part of) and some serious escape-on-a-quilt-with-a-magazine-under-a-tree time for me. To top that off, lunch at one of our favorite diners and shopping to boot.

That getaway was just the ticket!

"What a great idea," I said as I started a mental list to prepare for our jaunt: gather up car toys ... throw the tattered and comfy picnic quilt in the van ... stash my latest unread issue of *Today's Christian Woman* in my tote bag ...

"Oh, no."

Kurt could tell by my voice that a reality check had just stuck a long, rusty pin in my bubble of excitement.

"I just remembered. Lindsey has a birthday party to go to tomorrow. It's that skating party she's been counting down to. When I RSVP'd last week, I told Whitney's mom how tickled Lindsey was to be invited, and that she would definitely be there ... I just don't know if we should bail out like that ... I'm sure they've made plans for a certain number of children ... ?" I half-stated, half-asked, trying to ignore the image in my mind of a mom who had probably been up until midnight the night before counting out cupcakes and bundling up party favors for each child who would be at the party. I secretly hoped the doubt in my voice had given Kurt enough latitude to overrule my objection. But no go. That do-the-right-thing angel must have hopped from my shoulder over to his.

"Yeah," he said. "You're right. Well ... can't be helped."

We got over the disappointment of not being able to make our spontaneous southward trek that Saturday and after a couple of additional failed attempts, we did manage to escape a few weeks later. To finally work it out, we simply marked the date on the calendar as if it was a play we had tickets to attend, a meeting we had committed to lead, or a project we had promised to help with. The day turned out to be everything I had hoped it would be—a delicious and restful retreat with three of my favorite people in the world—despite the lacking element of spontaneity.

Planning Pays

That episode gently initiated us into the world of school-age parenthood, in which kids begin to develop a circle of friends of their own, engage in extracurricular activities, and juggle heavier homework schedules. It also taught us a valuable lesson: Planning family time together takes just that—planning.

Commitment and a certain amount of sacrifice are in order too. For example, in making our plans for the Hot Springs outing, we realized while we studied our calendar that unless we wanted to postpone the trip until sometime next year, someone in our family would have to miss something. As it turned out, Nick missed a project workday but by planning ahead, we had given him a chance to let his teammates know and to arrange to bring his share of the project home to work on there.

Dinner Dates

Another mom—whose kids are grown now—says protecting her family's dinnertime was a great way she found to put family first. Bonnie Skinner, author of *Making Family Memories: A Family Night Planner*, always considered "the dinner hour ... almost sacred."

"I fought tooth and nail to keep that for our family until they left for college. We wanted to be sure that we took advantage of the time that we had when our kids were young," she says. "I know my kids thought I was some sort of a fanatic, but we really made a superhuman effort to have that time around the table.

"I can't say that it was always just this wonderful conversation ... but we did it. We were there and the kids knew that we were wanting to know what was going on in their lives, and we were praying together at the end of the meal."

With responsibilities and activities tugging at each family member at nearly every turn, it seems to be tougher now than ever to keep that dinner hour intact. In a society that accommodates working parents by scheduling baseball practices, art lessons, and Scout meetings for 5:30 or 6:00 rather than 3:30 or 4:00, the dinner hour can easily get lost in the shuffle. Especially in families with more than one busy school-ager, eating in shifts at the kitchen counter often becomes a way of life.

But Bonnie and other experts say that fiercely protecting the family dinner hour is likely to yield more than a warm, fuzzy feeling each evening. She cites one recent study which "showed that adolescents whose parents ate dinner with them five times a week or more were least likely to be on drugs or in trouble with the law." Another report indicates that "table talk" helps build children's literacy, and yet another study shows that one of the common denominators in a group of out-standing students was regular family dinners.

Besides trying to schedule her kids' activities and events around the family's dinnertime, Bonnie says another way she kept the mealtime meeting intact was simply to take the phone off the hook.

"It got really hard when they were teenagers because the phone is their lifeline," she says. "But that was just what we did."

Bonnie says she recently got to see some of the fruits of her efforts of all those years: After trying for about an hour and a half to reach her married daughter in another town, she finally got through. "I said, 'I called earlier and your line was busy.' Kristy said, 'Yeah, we took the phone off because we were eating dinner.' I loved it! So it made a big impression on them."

Family Night

The Skinners' commitment to building family unity spilled over from the dinner hour into an even more creative way to spend time with their kids. They started planning regularly scheduled "Family Nights" when their children were very young.

"[We felt] that we just needed to carve out some

special time to play with the kids and to really focus on them," she says. "... We wanted family to be a priority and so we just started using this little booklet that we found. It had some ideas on what to do for a family night. We just took the booklet and continued to do it over the years.

"They really, from the very beginning, liked it. It was just part of our life.

"We went through different stages. For a while when they're little, you can just say, 'Friday night's family night.' They're not going anywhere anyway. It's harder for Mom and Dad to carve it out than it is for the kids at that point. But when the kids get older and they start getting involved in organized sports, or whatever, then it really becomes a challenge because of their schedules.

"If you start with your kids when they're young so that they like it, they enjoy it, they look forward to it, then there will be a history there and they will want to do it. But even if you start when they're a little older, if the kids are already in grade school, I don't think it takes too many times for the kids to catch on to 'This is really fun.'

"If they can have two or three fun family nights, then you have them until about 14 or 15, and then their peers become so important it's just hard. At that point, it's a matter of saying 'This is part of what we do. So we'll work with you so that we can have this time.' It was just supremely important to us to have that time with the family.

"I think there's that need in the children to have time with Mom and Dad, their undivided attention. Not that we don't give it to them other times, but just to have that special time where [we say], 'You guys are a priority.'

"We used [family nights] as a time to build memories, as a time to build into their lives a strong positive self-concept and also as a teaching time."

Bonnie and her husband seized family nights as an opportunity to address basic Christian issues as well as those relating to character qualities or current events. The benefits of such family time counter a trend in society that shows family members becoming more and more scattered and independent, thus less connected.

"Many families are all going on their own little track and don't have a chance to relate as a family," Bonnie says. "For some people, their one or two weeks of vacation a year is the only time they really interact with the family. But we feel like the message is clear that if we don't spend time with [the kids] and make our family a fun place to be, they will become more and more dependent on their peers. We feel that is one of the big benefits of having a regular family night, to give them a sense of family identity and unity." (See Appendix A) [1]

Family Traditions

Daily prayer times, nightly bedtime stories, Sunday lunches at Grandma's, spring and fall barbecues. Every family needs these kinds of predictable rituals that give kids a sense of security and family unity. Such activities don't have to be elaborate, spectacular, or set against an exciting holiday backdrop. They just have to be enjoyable and dependable. It's okay to drop some family traditions along the way as your family's tastes and circumstances change. Just make sure you add others in their place. For example, as one family's grade-schoolers grew into teens, they swapped their Easter egg-dyeing sessions for an annual spring visit to see a nearby outdoor theater production of the life of Christ.

Homes are made of humans, and humans aren't perfect. Even if we put into practice every marriage-enhancing trick, each parenting tip, all the family life-enriching strategies we run across, we're powerless to build a solid, loving home apart from God. "For no one can lay any foundation other than the one already laid, which is Jesus Christ" (1 Corinthians 3:11). He alone offers our families the home that really matters, for "our citizenship is in heaven" (Philippians 3:20). And He alone can empower us to create secure homes that "will be a refuge" for our children (Proverbs 14:26).

chapter 2

Hospitality: Home Is a Verb

> "Offer hospitality to one
> another without grumbling."
> —1 Peter 4:9

A Midwestern mom phoned in to a radio program in support of stay-at-home moms. "I've got six teenage boys downstairs and most of their moms work," she said. "They could go to any of their empty homes after school—unsupervised—but they like to come here to hang out. They like me being here, even though I pretty much leave them alone."

She said all it usually takes to entice them to stick around is a little conversation and a batch of caramel apples from time to time.

Hospitality isn't merely about lighting a couple candles when company's coming for dinner—although that's nice. More important, it's the perpetual motion of using our homes to serve God and all those who cross our thresholds—including muddy Boy Scout troop #42 members, the rowdy 10-year-old neighbor, and the kids—all 23—from Mr. Strommer's science class who need a place to conduct a "stinky" experiment.

As moms, we do these things often, without realizing the impact our gestures of hospitality can make on the young lives crisscrossing through our yards and parking for popcorn in our dens.

"It's really important for us to be hospitable to our kids' friends," says Holly Schurter of Illinois, mother of

" I could not imagine not being home for my kids. Even my oldest, I feel, needs to have her mom here when she comes home. I call it 'keeping her grounded to the earth.' All of her friends know this is where they are welcome to come over and hang out. It has helped me get to know her friends better, and they also have another adult they can count on for advice or to just talk to. **"**

—April, mother of four

eight who shares the bounty of her mothering experience through workshops. "Especially these days, I think a lot of children don't get the kind of family experiences that we can offer as Christian families. We have something special— the love of our Savior, Jesus—that changes our lives and relationships. A lot of kids don't get the opportunity to see that kind of love in action within a family setting."

Christ says, "... whoever welcomes a little child like this in My name welcomes Me" (Matthew 18:5). Although they're all "precious in His sight," being hospitable to kids isn't always as simple (or as rewarding) as being hospitable to grown-ups. The under-12 set doesn't necessarily know how to graciously acknowledge a hostess' efforts. In fact, many moms have seen how quickly playing waitress to a ravenous pack of neighborhood playmates can leave them feeling less like the happy-go-lucky Kool-Aid moms of the 70s' TV commercials and more like threadbare day-care center doormats.

"When our kids were all very small, we lived in a neighborhood where there were a lot of small children," Holly recalls. "I remember one afternoon looking out into our side yard, there were 17 kids there. Our house and another house down the street were kind of the neighborhood playgrounds.

"At times that was hard," she says. "That carries all kinds of questions like: Do you feed all those kids? Do you let them come in the house? What about when they need to go to the bathroom? Wash their hands? When they get hurt, what do you do?"

The best strategy for settling these kinds of issues and converting child-care chaos into backyard bliss is to think through possible situations and ways to handle them before they arise.

"I don't think that God requires us in every instance to give everything that we have all at once," she says. That's why it's important to set some boundaries.

"Bring up those issues with your husband and talk about it and bring it up with your kids and talk about it. Let them know what some of the issues are so they can help you. If they are helping you enforce it, it goes a lot better. But if your kids are among the ones saying, 'Gee, Mom, why can't we ...' then you're ready to kill them!"

As mayor of your own corner of Munchkinland, you're entitled to tailor such laws and bylaws to suit your family's lifestyle.

Kurt and Nick have spent hundreds of hours and lots of dollars perfecting their miniature train set-up that has taken over our garage. So—as enticing as it is—the system's off-limits to playmates who might not realize the fragility and value of the project. Maybe your kids know the riding lawnmower in the backyard is not a toy but the new kid on the block might not realize its potential danger. From "Don't ride your bikes through the next-door neighbor's yard" to "Always empty out your shoes before you come inside after you've been in the sandbox," clearly outline rules and boundaries, and teach your kids how to pass them on to guests—politely. When setting playtime boundaries, consider limitations and freedoms regarding the following.

Time

"My times are in Your hands".

Psalm 31:15

Do you have younger children who nap at certain times of the day? You might want to call your yard off-limits during that time span. Also think about the dinner hour. "We had a rule that when the kids came in for dinner, everybody had to go home," Holly says. That was partly for safety's sake (Mom and Dad at the dinner table means no watchful eyes on the crew outside), but she says it also encouraged playmates to go home and spend time with their own families.

Feeding the Masses

"If anyone gives a cup of cold water to one of these little ones because he is My disciple, I tell you the truth, he will certainly not lose his reward."

Matthew 10:42

Does that mean we feed and water each of these kids who drift through our gates day in and day out? It depends.

"You can't afford to feed them all every day," Holly notes. So she suggests two tactics: "I tried to find snacks that were nutritious and not expensive, and I tried to offer them on an irregular basis so the kids didn't know when I was going to come out with a snack or when I wasn't. I didn't want to set up an expectation."

Tidbits like crackers and peanut butter (ask about food allergies first), pretzels, and fruit juices are practical. Other inexpensive snacktime ideas include popcorn, inexpensive cookies such as animal crackers or vanilla wafers, Popsicles, graham crackers, Jell-O, marshmallows, dry cereal, and even just plain water. Holly says she sometimes served water with a little lemon in it and found it "surprising how kids appreciate things like that sometimes. You can also put pretzels in a little paper cup with a few raisins or something sprinkled in it and the kids think they've been treated so well. You can do special things to make kids feel like they're really honored guests."

Another hint: Small (bathroom-size) paper cups are great for passing out drinks, and coffee filters—especially the cone-shaped ones—make great inexpensive snack holders.

First Aid

"... and when he saw him, he took pity on him. He went to him and bandaged his wounds ... and took care of him."
Luke 10:33-34

A thud, a crying wail, then the thunder of footsteps rushing to the back door. Those sounds can tighten icy fingers of fear around a mom's heart. Who got hurt, and what happened? What should you do next? Keep a first-aid kit handy to fix scraped knees and bumped elbows. But for anything more serious, call or send for the child's parents.

Inside-Outside

"Let the little children come to Me ...
for the kingdom of heaven
belongs to such as these."

Matthew 19:14

Theirs may be the kingdom of heaven but we know we can't keep our homes very heavenly with kids running in and out hour after hour. The revolving-door dilemma has plagued moms since before the days of Wally and the Beav. Do you let the kids play inside? Even if you just vacuumed and mopped? Even if flies are buzzing in line to get into your kitchen? Even if you have little ones napping inside? And what is it about kids that makes them want to play outside the minute they've set up the entire Barbie household in the middle of your den floor? Think about the ins and outs of how you want to handle this scenario and let your word be law (except for emergencies, of course). Some parameters might include allowing the kids to play inside if they stay in the bedroom (or the playroom, or the den, etc.). Or letting them play inside anytime they have two or less compadres. Or never letting them play inside when you're trying to cook dinner.

A Legacy of Hospitality

Showing hospitality to our kids and their friends doesn't just fulfill a biblical mandate (see 1 Peter 4:8–9 and Romans 12:13), it also teaches our kids—by example, which happens to be one of the best ways they learn—how to be hospitable as well.

"If we don't offer ... hospitality to children, how will our kids feel like they can offer hospitality as they get older?" Holly notes. "If they see it from the time they're little on up, and we allow them to help with that and extend hospitality to their friends, it becomes a natural thing for them as they get older. They have a real, deep understanding of what it costs and what it means to offer [hospitality]."

With many of her kids having now reached adulthood, Holly has already been blessed with the privilege of seeing some of the fruits of her efforts throughout the years. "Now that our kids are in college, their friends still feel welcome to come and roost and visit and talk. So it's something that makes me feel good. It started back there in the yard when all these kids would come to our house."

Basic Training

We can teach our kids how to be hospitable not only by our example, but by getting them involved in preparations for guests and by rehearsing scenarios.

Being Prepared

One secret of being a hostess at-the-ready, Holly says, is to keep at least one area of the house constantly cleared away for the possible drop-in. In some homes, it might be the formal living room; in others, a couple of nice chairs in a cozy corner of the living room might be off-limits to clutter. Recruit the kids' cooperation in keeping these areas junk-free by letting them use the space for their guests as well. That way, Holly says, "they get a feeling for why that space is important."

Another way to prepare for unexpected visitors is by keeping something special in the pantry or freezer off-limits until the need arises. Because a nice tin of cookies tucked away in a remote corner can be a mighty strong temptation for hungry tykes, rally the troops' cooperation by letting them know that those cookies are "reserved" for special guests.

Rehearsing Scenarios

"A lot of times we expect our kids to be hospitable, but we don't show them how," Holly says. "When we knew we were having company, I would let the kids help me get ready. I began role-playing with them while we would do the work. I would say, 'Okay, somebody's at the door. It's Aunt Grizelda. How are you going to introduce her to somebody?' Then when those situations would come up, they had already tried it with me. They were more comfortable doing it with guests because they had practiced it with me. It's not a guarantee that our kids will be perfectly well-mannered all the time, but it certainly increases the odds."

Opening Your Heart to Others

(Or Don't Let Yucky Carpet Inhibit the Hostess in You)

I've joked among my friends that I can't have many "to-do's"—showers, fellowships, cookouts—at my house until we replace our 15-year-old chocolate brown, worn-out carpet (an event that has been postponed for three years because it's just so expensive, but hallelujah, by the time you read this we should finally be treading on some nice turf in a shade and fabric from this decade). We all laugh, but I'm the only one who really knows how I've let my worn carpet hinder my hospitality to kids and grown-ups alike.

But Holly points out that hospitality's not about me, my ugly carpet, mismatched glasses that may be lurking in my cabinets, or my laundry-heaped sofa. It's about keeping my heart, not my home, ready to minister to my guests' needs with God's gracious love and hospitality.

"In my case, we had so many small children, our house was never clean," Holly says. "But did God call me to be Martha Stewart? Obviously not. He called me to be who I am here in this place, under these circumstances."

So she adopted a gracious attitude that says:

> This is the best I have to offer today.
> I'll clear the laundry off
> and I'll put it in a basket and ask,
> 'Would you like a cup of tea?'
> when guests pop by.

"That way, the focus is not on me, or what I have. The focus is on you. You're my guest. God has brought you to my door.

"Our kids need to learn that you want to offer the best you have and that means you want to keep things picked up as much as possible. But realistically, that's not always going to be what the house looks like when people come. So get your mind off yourself and what's wrong with you and put your mind on the other person and why God has brought them to you."

Gee, after hearing Holly's take on hospitality, I think I'll toss some throw rugs over the torn spots and invite some friends and their kids over for dinner Friday night ...

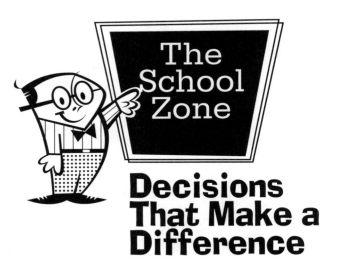

part II

The School Zone

Decisions That Make a Difference

chapter 3

Choosing the Right School

"We felt that our children could learn more at home than at [traditional] school."
—*Mary, mother of Matthew, 5, and Elisabeth, 3*

"We love the Christian values [of a private Christian school]. They teach the kids to be humble and kind, and things that we try to teach them at home are reinforced there. We know that our values are extending to the school. That's a wonderful thing."
—*Andrea Batchelor, mother of Richard, 11, David, 8½, and Matthew, 5*

"We've felt called as a family to evangelism—to make a difference in the world. Having our kids attend public schools while under a strong Christian influence at home and in youth groups has helped their faith and values mature."
—*Susan Alexander Yates*[2]

Three sets of parents, three sets of children, three sets of reasoning behind crucial educational choices.

Toss up the topic during a play date powwow and you'll be amazed at the variety of conflicting opinions you'll hear: A couple of moms will tell their public school horror stories while another confesses that she's simply not up to the task of teaching her kids at home. She says she looks forward to the diversity and opportunities available to her kids through the public school system. Another mom observes that private schools seem to offer the best of both worlds, while yet another, rolling her eyes, says, "Right, if you can afford it."

The milestones of the preschool years give us plenty of experience in making key decisions regarding the upbringing of our kids. After all, we sorted our way through the breast-or-bottle issue; we analyzed the time-out versus spanking debate; we settled the stay-at-home/work-outside-the home matter; and we assumed a comfortable position on whether or not to bring baby into bed with us. But successfully negotiating our way through that maze of choices just means it's time to graduate to the next biggie: How do we best educate our kids?

The choices aren't all that simple anymore.

For example, it's no longer just a matter of public school versus private school. More than a dozen states have implemented choices ranging from charter schools to magnet schools. And homeschool has, within the past 15 years, charged to the head of the class for many families. Because all these perspectives can seem overwhelming, here's some basic information to help you do your homework in researching this complex school project. As you dig into the specifics, keep these points in mind:

God's Word gives us direction on every issue we'll ever confront in life, but He doesn't spell out any specific "thou shalts" regarding our kids' formal education. He knows the specific needs of each of our families, so we as parents "in charge" undergird each step we take toward a decision with prayer, prayer, and more prayer. "If any of you lacks wisdom, he should ask God, who gives generously to all without finding fault, and it will be given to him" (James 1:5).

 Our decision doesn't have to be written in permanent ink. One mom sent her kids to a private Christian school during their early elementary years when she felt they would reap the most benefits from small classes, great teacher-student ratios, and thorough biblical instruction. She felt this gave them a solid springboard into the public school system. Another mom has her kids in public school "because it gives them an outlet from me, teaches them to get along with others, and challenges them in a way that I don't think I could." However, she stresses that she would change her decision in a heartbeat "if my kids' needs weren't being met or if their safety became an issue."

All schools can't be lumped into the same category. Different types of public schools may have different formats or emphases. Private schools—even Christian private schools—often vary dramatically on all points, from religious teachings to academic philosophy. Homeschool programs and curricula offer a diverse range of options designed to meet a variety of needs. A thorough investigation is the only way to avoid basing this important decision on an unrealistic set of characteristics.

If you haven't yet defined your personal education philosophy, this is the time to do it. Discuss with your spouse exactly what you both expect from your children's education. Do you place a strong emphasis on academic excellence? Do you desire an educational experience to be rounded out by a variety of social and extracurricular activities? Do you value racial and economic diversity? How do the arts and creativity figure in to your expectations? Do you believe values, morals, and religious instruction should be integrated into a formal learning setting? How do you feel about interaction/separation of ages? Develop an outline of your conclusions and keep it as a checklist while you explore your options.

Homeschool:
Education in a Class by Itself

Certainly the idea of homeschooling is nothing new. This timeless practice of teaching one's children at home is the oldest educational forum known to humankind. Why, then, is it so surprising that as many as 1.2 million American kids are homeschooled, according to the Home School Legal Defense Association, which reports that figure is rising each year at a rate of about 25 percent?

Parents who decide to homeschool generally do so for one or more of the following reasons:

Religious—They want the foundations of their children's faith and beliefs to be reinforced in every part of their lives, including formal education.

Academic—They may not be confident that the education offered their child at a public or private school meets the standards they expect.

Social/Safety—They are troubled about issues such as violence, drugs, gangs, and negative peer behavior in public schools.

Homeschool families often echo the following refrains:

"We want to have control over what our kids are learning."

"We are obligated to fulfill the biblical instruction to teach our children." (See Deuteronomy 4:9; 6:7-8.)

"We wanted to offer a one-on-one, customized educational setting for our kids."

"We want to enhance our family unity."

"We needed to offer a safer and more desirable alternative to public schools."

Homeschool ... Tuition?

Homeschooling sounds like a pretty economical educational route, and it generally is. While textbooks and supplies do cost money, expenses can be kept at bay with strategies such as buying used materials and sharing supplies with other homeschool families. However, parents pay a rather steep tuition in another currency: time and commitment.

Homeschooling takes many forms, from a daily structured routine to a flexible, free style of learning.

Either way, it requires a major quantity of time—spent on both the actual teaching and on planning lessons and gathering supplies. It also requires, at times, a superhuman ability to stay on task despite or amid interruptions ranging from a ringing phone to housework to holiday preparations to keeping siblings occupied. Wearing both "mom" and "teacher" hats calls for lots of organization, a willingness to step into a different role of authority in a child's life, and some fancy footwork to keep a kid's education on track.

Not for Everyone

As attractive as many of the "pros" for homeschooling may be, obviously many parents don't consider it an option for reasons such as a perceived lack of socialization, younger siblings to care for, or a lack of qualifications.

"I have tossed around the idea of homeschooling," says Amanda. "I often push it to the back of my mind for two major reasons, one being that I am afraid I would not have enough patience to teach my son properly, and the second being that my son would miss being with his classmates. He is doing very well in his class and I am happy with that."

Indeed, homeschooling may not be the right direction for your family if

- You can't stand the thought of doing it. Homeschooling requires a consistent commitment of time and energy and if your heart's not in it, chances are you won't succeed.

- You have even more compelling reasons to choose public school or private school—perhaps a child with learning problems or special needs that you simply are not equipped to meet.

- You have prayed about it and feel no conviction to consider it further.
- Your spouse is not supportive. "I think it's important to have your spouse's support for homeschooling because if you don't, and you have a bad day and need to vent some of it, you can't do it to your husband," says Jaz, who homeschooled her daughter when she was in the fourth grade. "The kids pick up on that subtle negativity, even if he doesn't say anything overt. Also, I would have liked my husband to teach my daughter some things (he's a programmer, has a degree in music, and is an amateur linguist), but I couldn't get him to commit."

If, after weighing the pros and cons of the issue, you decide to homeschool, know that many people have misconceptions about homeschooling. So when you're investigating the topic, talk to parents who homeschool or who have done so in the past. Don't ask parents who have never homeschooled and who would never homeschool in a million years; they won't have anything concrete or valuable to offer.

If you take this route, find a homeschool support network in your area. They can answer your questions about curricula, tell you about any local organized sports teams and/or extracurricular organizations,

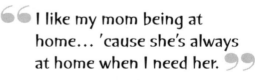

I like my mom being at home... 'cause she's always at home when I need her.

—Laurel, age 10 ½

offer you the opportunity to share resources, and point you to some great school supply sources.

Check with the following organizations:

American Homeschool Association
PO Box 3142
Palmer, AK 99645-3142 (907-746-1336)
e-mail: AHA@home-ed-magazine.com
http://www.home-ed-magazine.com/AHA/aha.html

Home School Legal Defense Association
PO Box 3000
Purcellville, VA 20134
540-338-5600
http://www.hslda.org
Membership in HSLDA provides legal information and, if necessary, representation for homeschooling issues. Other services include the National Center for Home Educators and the bimonthly magazine, *The Home School Court Report.*

National Home Education Research Institute
PO Box 13939
Salem, OR 97309
503-364-1490
http://www.nheri.org
NHERI does research and provides facts and statistics about homeschooling for dealing with curious or critical family members, legislators, courts of law, neighbors, and the media. NHERI also consults with homeschool organizations.

The Teaching Home
Box 20219
Portland, OR 97294-0219
503-253-9633

Private Schools:
First-Class Education

Some private schools build character and develop moral integrity and values. Some give kids the academic foundation they'll need to land on the college campus of their choice. And some just give kids more of the "extras"—from shiny new equipment and specialized elective courses to small classes and plush surroundings. Regardless of what they expect in return for the tuition they pay for their children's education, many parents—whose children make up more than 10 percent of the nation's students—opt to go private.

You won't need an advanced degree to understand your options when you explore private school as an alternative for your children, but a little basic education about the different types of schools that fall into this category might start you off on the right foot:

Montessori schools are "based on an approach to education that emphasizes the potential of a young child," according to the principal of one Montessori school. The programs feature a self-paced curriculum based on the idea that children learn by doing. Buzzwords within this style of education include "holistic" and "child-centered" learning. Montessori students are encouraged to take control of their own behavior in order to develop an inner discipline. For example, if a child becomes disruptive during an activity, the teacher might give the child the choice of either staying involved in the activity and being quiet or leaving the activity to work on something else. This learning approach often means no grades.

Roman Catholic schools are educating approximately half of America's students who attend nonpublic schools. Most of these parochial schools emphasize discipline, respect for authority, and traditional values. Laypeople have largely replaced the nuns as teachers in recent years and many non-Catholics (about 17 percent of those enrolled) find these schools appealing.

Christian schools, according to one source, are the fastest growing variety of private school in the nation. The National Center for Education Statistics indicates that more than 600,000 students attend Christian schools, which often incorporate a strong emphasis on promoting Christian values in the classroom. "My desire (as well as my husband's) is for our children to be 100 percent surrounded by God's teaching," says Tula, mom of three who is pleased with the education her kids are receiving at a church-operated Christian school. "That begins at home, and continues into church and school." Bible study and worship are often an integral part of the Christian school curriculum. For example, one private Christian elementary school features a morning Bible class as well as a mid-day "praise break" during which kids sing and participate in a worship service. Many Christian schools are open to children of all faiths, in part because they use the school as an evangelism tool.

College prep or private independent schools strive to give students the academic foundation that will pave their way to the college campus of their choice. Although a primary focus of many such schools revolves around each student's academic development, they also emphasize nurturing certain basic character traits such as honesty and integrity. These schools frequently cater to the economic and social "elite," and can come with a breathtakingly high price tag.

Sticker Shock

Because of the pricey nature of many private schools, it's easy for parents who are just starting their research to get a case of sticker shock. For many parents, it's a struggle to write that tuition check each month. But because parents generally decide to place their children in private school for a specific reason—whether it's safety concerns, a particular curriculum, a desire for spiritual/religious instruction or a specific discipline—they regard tuition as an investment in their children's lives.

"They do it because they want a feeling of choice and control over their child's educational experience," one private school superintendent says. "They pay because they're serious about education. They're not serious about education because they pay."

One note might help soften the blow to the old pocketbook if you're leaning toward private school: Most schools offer financial assistance in the form of scholarships and/or discounts for siblings attending the same school.

Getting in

It's one thing to decide where you'd like your child to go to school; it's another to arrange to foot the bill, and quite another to actually secure a spot on the school's roster. Most schools conduct re-enrollment in the spring to give students currently attending first priority. In some cases, this doesn't leave much room for new faces on campus next fall.

The application procedures and requirements for attendance vary from school to school, so contact the admissions offices to get information. They'll probably want to look at your child's past academic records, teacher recommendations, financial information, discipline history, and behavioral profile. Your child may be required to take an entrance test and/or be interviewed.

The whole process might seem a bit intimidating, leaving parents to wonder whether their child will be able to gain admission to the school of their choice. But the headmaster of one private academy says his school doesn't have unrealistic expectations. And another says his admissions personnel don't necessarily take just the straight-A students. He says his faculty looks at each applicant's profile with an eye toward desirable characteristics such as leadership skills. "I do think there are a lot of misconceptions about private schools," he says. "You'll find some pretty common folk ... from a lot of walks of life."

If you are exploring the private school alternative, ask the following questions about any schools you are considering:

What is the religious affiliation/philosophy?

What is the teacher to student ratio?

What is the educational level of the faculty?

How much is tuition? Is there a financial aid or payment plan?

Do other expenses or fees crop up through the year (parent-teacher organization membership dues, book and supply fees, activity fees, etc.)?

What extracurricular activities are offered?

What type of curriculum is used?

What accreditation does the school have?

Public Schools:
Education for the People

About 90 percent of American children attend public elementary school. The National Center for Education Statistics says it's the leading educational choice for three reasons: parents feel it provides a better academic environment; they want to take advantage of special academic courses; and they desire the convenience offered by the public school system.

More Choices Than Ever Before

Whether you're a newcomer to your area or a native, if you choose to go public, you've got to learn a lot in order to take advantage of the flexibility offered to public elementary-schoolers in many of the nation's districts. Public neighborhood schools are still an option for most American families but recent changes have reshaped public education to offer more choices.

Charter Schools:
Private Education for the Price of Public

Since 1992, approximately 500 charter schools have opened nationwide. Charter schools generally operate under an agreement, or charter, between the school's sponsors and state or local officials with the goal of boosting student performance and raising academic standards. State laws differ in how they define charter schools, but some common characteristics include:

Charter schools have no religious affiliation.

They do not charge tuition.

They operate independently from their districts while adhering to the guidelines set forth in the charter.

Magnet Schools:
Specialized Study

In addition to offering a standard elementary curriculum, magnet schools typically give students the chance to explore specialized areas of study such as international studies, arts, or math and science. For example, at one magnet school, students are regularly treated to visits from guests from other countries, and they plan many multicultural activities and events. And at another, kids can see the constellations while learning about astronomy and science by visiting the on-campus "sky lab," an inflatable, room-sized planetarium.

To find out more about your local public schools, contact your school district headquarters and your state Department of Education. You can also check out the U.S. Charter Schools website at http://www.uscharter-schools.org/ and the National Public School Locator, which offers a searchable database of basic information about the schools in your area at http://nces.ed.gov/ccd-web/school/school.asp.

You'll also want to

Visit with the principal and teachers at the school your child might be attending to get a feel for the atmosphere, educational philosophy, attitude toward parental involvement, discipline policies, dress codes, and safety measures.

Attend open houses.

Talk to members of your church whose children attend that school.

Check into the district superintendent's philosophy/track record.

Consider the district's rating.

Check into busing policies and issues.

 School Daze:

Mom's Primer
for the
Primary Years

> "Let the wise listen and add to their learning, and let the discerning get guidance ..."—Proverbs 1:5

Swallowing sobs as I made my way through the blurred parking lot after leaving Nick in a room full of strangers on his first day of kindergarten, I didn't feel I would ever be able to climb out from under the blanket of grief smothering me. I wasn't mourning over the big issues many journalists write about in touching back-to-school columns in thick, slick magazines and Sunday newspapers: I didn't feel my firstborn wasn't going to be needing me anymore—I remembered enough about being school-age to know that you never quit needing Mom. I didn't worry about my diminishing role in his world. I wanted him to have a circle of friends and I knew I planned to continue to be enough of a hands-on mom that I wouldn't yield my influence on him for a long time to come. And I wasn't simply feeling sentimental in the "where did the time go ... just yesterday I was bringing him home from the hospital" sense. I had, after all, become a stay-at-home mom to prevent ever having to say such a thing. I knew good and well where the time had gone. He had spent it with me, day after day, being rocked and raised, discipled and disciplined in his home, in his yard, at his pace, and according to his personality.

I was sending him off to school knowing I had given him the very best—and most—of what I had to offer during the years I had him in my complete care.

No, the source of my grief was much more basic: I was just going to miss him so much. The little boy who had rocked my world and shaken our family's priorities into place five years earlier would no longer be folding bomber planes at 10:00 A.M. or building forts in the den after a chicken nugget lunch. He wouldn't be holding Lindsey's other hand as the three of us walked into the grocery store to do our shopping. He wouldn't be spouting out colorfully turned words and phrases throughout the day that would send me running to my little blue notebook.

He would be parked at his desk in the kid-colored classroom, sponging up new info about his world, making Pilgrim hats and terrariums, and monkeying around on the playground while his 3-year-old sister and I tried to sort out a new structure for our lives. We were Nick-less, and it felt just awful.

I wish I could say that a life-changing revelation came later that day to dissolve my grief. Or that the replay two years later when Lindsey became a kindergartner was easier. But I can't. The drama of separating from kids we've spent practically every hour with since they were born can't be downplayed. I can, however, say that we adjusted. I'm sure some moms do so more quickly than others. For me, the grief crept away in small degrees as I discovered that back-to-school wasn't synonymous with total separation—the exodus of Nick left a surplus of time and attention from which Lindsey benefited—and that, hey, it felt pretty good to have some more time to call my own.

As I came out of the fog of sadness, I began to see clearly that this transition was signaling a God-given promotion in my career of stay-at-home motherhood. My kids were being launched from their home pad to explore the "real world." I was blasting off alongside them into a mothering job that carried extra duties, an expanded territory, and an ever-increasing crew of colleagues that now included not only fellow moms but teachers and faculty, gym instructors and baseball coaches. This advancement called for sharp people-management skills, acute attention to details, a knack for time management, and a thorough knowledge of problem-solving techniques. It also called for more prayer time to depend on God's faithful love and guidance.

So, intimidated as I was by the promotion, for the second time in my mothering career, I decided to do some on-the-job training. I found out everything I could to master the basics of school-age parenting.

Getting Ready for School

Whether the kids are starting kindergarten or fourth grade, sliding from summertime into school can be a jarring experience. Here are some off-to-school "do's and don'ts" that will prevent mental meltdown as we prepare ourselves, our kids, and even our homes, for the big change:

Do

- Establish a regular bedtime at least a week or two before school starts.
- Practice the getting-up and getting-ready routine at least a few days before D-day. (A cool new alarm clock for each school-bound child might be a great "back-to-school" present.)

- Begin "selling" school by mentioning things to look forward to: "The kindergartners always go to the pumpkin patch in the fall ... won't that be fun?" "Can you believe this is the year you will start learning how to read?" "Third-grade classes get to take turns at flagpole duty."
- If you're not homeschooling, discuss getting to school. If you'll be carpooling, go over all the details of who's driving, and on what days. Make sure your children can easily recognize the other drivers' vehicles in the parking lot or traffic lanes. If your kids will be riding the bus, visit the bus stop and go over details  of the entire bus experience. Find out the driver's name, the bus number, and which friends will be riding the bus. Go over bus and traffic safety rules.
- Take care of dental, eye doctor, and pediatric check-ups before school begins. We made the mistake of putting off Lindsey's eye exam too long and, as a result, she got her first pair of glasses right at the beginning of kindergarten—two traumatic events for such a small child to handle at once.
- Start setting up the "school zones": hang hooks by the back door for backpacks; set up files or notebooks to catch each kids' notes, permission slips, etc.; designate drawers or boxes to collect each child's "keepsake" work. If you're planning to homeschool, organize materials and start setting up and equipping learning areas.
- Review names and numbers your kids should remember—home, Dad at work, Grandma, carpool drivers. (For younger children, print the

information on an index card, laminate it, and attach it to the backpack.)

- Review last year's yearbook (if you have one) to remind your kids of familiar faces and names.
- Get your lunch plan ready. Talk to "lunch takers" about what they'll like packed in their lunch, and gather plastic baggies, napkins, straws, and milk money into one corner of the kitchen to save steps as you pack. Talk to your "cafeteria tray" eaters about how to carry a loaded tray through a crowd of kids (practice in your own kitchen if they're nervous), and go over the school's lunchtime routine.
- Start a habit of laying out school clothes the night before.
- Make school preparations fun and special: plan a mother-daughter school-clothes shopping trip; set up a special box to collect sale-purchased school supplies throughout the summer; start a tradition of picking out a new backpack or lunchbox every "even" or "odd" year.
- Talk about how you plan to be involved at school if you're not teaching the kids at home: "I'll be helping Mrs. Johnson in the library each Wednesday." "I'm going to be Mrs. Cook's room mother this year."
- Set up a school-mom station. Keep a note pad, pen, envelopes, and a supply of money (quarters, ones, and an occasional five) in one spot at the kitchen desk to jot notes to teachers, rustle up popcorn money, and fill out school photo orders. When sending money to school, it's good to put it in a sealed envelope clearly labeled with the student's name, teacher's name, and purpose.

Don't

- Emphasize how much you'll miss your kids during the days.
- Express worry or complain about certain teachers: "I sure hope you don't get Mrs. Weasel. I hear she yells a lot."
- Make light of comments that reveal your kids' concerns. Instead, encourage them to talk about their worries and guide them to possible solutions to their anticipated problems.
- Over-schedule after-school time.
- Plan unusual or potentially disruptive activities early in the year. (This isn't the time to schedule your non-emergency foot surgery, for example.)

The Home-School Connection Counts

Plainly put, kids whose parents plug into their kids' public and private education do better in school. They perform better on standardized tests, adjust better socially, report higher levels of self-confidence, excel in math and science ... the list goes on. Here are some ways to strengthen our link to our kids' learning experiences:

1. Team Up with Teachers

As kids hop off school buses and tumble out of minivans on the first day of school, they aren't the only ones wondering what the next nine months hold. Behind each backpack-clad student stands an anxious mom and/or dad wondering the same thing.

As for me, I am certain of this: At the beginning of each school year, I get ready to fall in love again. No, I don't chuck my values—or my husband—out the window to run away to the Bahamas with the cable guy. I just know from years of experience that I tumble head over heels for my kids' teachers.

My little romance with teachers began in my own second-grade classroom, when jolly Mrs. White tickled her snaggle-toothed bunch of 7-year-olds into hysterics by colorfully defining the manure we were spreading on our vegetable garden. Other highlights of this amour have included a fascinated crush on Mrs. Miles, a Native American who gave my fourth-grade class ukulele lessons, and respectful adoration of Ms. Molett, a stern but loving nun who taught in public schools "way back when" it was okay to read a Bible verse to her class each morning.

As an adult, I had nearly forgotten about my tendency to fall in love with teachers until always-smiling Mrs. Jessup rekindled the flame by ushering my first grader across the life-changing threshold between "can't read" and "can read." All of a sudden this inquisitive, blue-eyed 6-year-old wasn't asking me to read to him; he was reading to ME!

To keep the sparks of romance crackling in our parent-teacher relationships, we can use some of the same tips that sustain a healthy marriage:

Avoid Comparisons

I don't react well when my husband says, "That's not how my mom always cooked spaghetti." So rather than screeching, "Mrs. Bailey always used to let Lindsey ...," we should guard our mouths and tongues to keep from calamity (Proverbs 21:23).

Show Respect

Even though some may not appear old enough to drive themselves to school each day (and they look younger every year!), teachers have worked hard to earn their spot at the head of the class. We hand them the reins of our kids' education, submit ourselves and our kids "for the Lord's sake" to their authority, and give them the respect God asks us to show everyone (1 Peter 2:13, 17). When a problem crops up—and it likely will at some point—rather than whining to fellow moms or destroying the teacher's trust by heading straight for the principal's office, we should first discuss it with the teacher, offering any possible solutions we see. We're likely to get a much speedier and more effective resolution when we don't alienate the teacher.

Make Dates

Dates with our mates allow us to reflect on our past and chart our future course. Dates with teachers—disguised as both teachers' conferences and impromptu discussions during field trips—give us occasion to celebrate our kids' accomplishments and to strategize ways to reach educational goals. "I try to keep very active lines of communication going between my son's teacher and me," says Gina. "I talk with her frequently ... not just at parent-teacher conferences."

Some conversation-starters for productive teacher conferences include

What has my child been learning and what will he be expected to learn in the coming weeks?

How is my child evaluated? How are grades determined?

What can I do at home to complement class work?

What can I do to help in the classroom?

Does my child need any special help such as speech therapy, tutoring, accelerated programs, etc., which I should check into?

When we need to discuss several issues with the teacher, a list of notes can help make sure we cover everything. Remember to approach these one-on-ones not only as information gatherers, but as information givers as well. This is the ideal setting to share personal information that can help the teacher understand our students' needs. Now is the time to mention that Charlie gets bored when he finishes his work early; that Maddie's self-confidence has blossomed since the teacher gave her the responsibility of being the regular "office runner." Also pass along any vital personal information—a death in the family, job change, illness, best friend moving away— that can cause your child to act differently in school. Letting teachers in on these developments can help them better help our kids.

Write Love Letters

With a job description almost as long and varied as that of a parent, teachers can always use the pen-and-paper equivalent of a pat on the back. So when they do special things for our kids—teaching them how to subtract, pulling a wobbly tooth, or giving a comforting hug to help conquer a teary bout with the Monday morning blues—we can take a few minutes to drop them a hearty "way to go!"

Give Tokens of Esteem

Teachers often spend more than a little of their own pocket money on their class in various ways throughout the year, not to mention the valuables they spend that aren't monetary: time, effort, care, concern. A little gift now and then can help show our appreciation for their beyond-the-call-of-duty deeds. And just as a little something from our spouse at times other than birthday and Christmas can brighten any day, spontaneity can do the trick for a tired teacher as well. Here are some tips:

Ask fellow teachers for ideas about special interests.

Pick up some note cards and stamps.

Consider pooling resources with other parents for more expensive items such as gift certificates to the school supply store or catalog, a set of books, etc.

Assemble a basket of personal goodies—bath salts, lotions, and potions; herbal teas and flavored coffees; nail-care supplies.

Find out what the teacher would like to have in the classroom that isn't in the budget—an electric pencil sharpener, computer software, a couple of beanbag chairs for the reading area, a certain set of reference books—and surprise her with them.

Offer to take over his lunchtime playground duty once a month.

Let your child decorate and personalize a canvas tote bag.

Purchase a classic video for his home library.

Give her homemade, handcrafted items.

Share food (canned goodies, fresh-baked cookies) in a decorative, reusable tin.

Send a potted plant for the teacher's classroom or home.

Cut flowers from your yard to brighten his desk.

Pray

My pastor's wife, an elementary school teacher, begins praying for her class during the summer, even before she knows which students she'll have. Following her cue, we can start praying for our teachers-to-be even before we know who they are. We may not know yet what our kids' teachers will do to send us into a love-struck tailspin, but we can usually be confident that our affections won't be misguided. After all, these teachers will have been hand-picked by a God who loves our kids even more than we do!

2. Offer Helping Hands in the Classroom and on Campus

Be a Teacher's Aide

Most teachers, no matter how efficient, can use an extra set of hands now and again. "I substitute in their classes when needed, drive for field trips, attend any special activities, and eat lunch with them periodically," says Tula, who knows how important it is to help her kids' teachers.

Another way to help teachers is to let them know we're willing to spend a few hours each week doing some of the following kinds of chores:

Performing "teacher's aide" stuff: grading papers, making copies, stapling pages, etc.

Reading with kids who need a little one-on-one attention

Reading to the class— "When Brad was in first grade," says Gina, "I started reading stories and chapter books to the class. The kids love the break from the routine, and I get such enjoyment from it!" She has continued that tradition into third grade, where she's now reading _The Chronicles of Narnia_ every Thursday morning. A gifted storyteller, her presentation mesmerizes the kids, gives the teacher a break, provides her with a weekly peek at the class and classroom routines, and presents her a rare opportunity to minister in the public classroom through the classic C. S. Lewis allegory.

Chaperoning field trips

Teaching the kids a hobby or skill——whether it's
Spanish, papier-mâché, or creative writing, teachers
will love the way you enhance their curriculum

Being a "room mom" who helps with parties, field trips, etc.

Taking a special new pet to visit the classroom

Campus Crusader

In a setting as vital and volatile as an elementary school, faculty and staff appreciate any help a parent's willing to offer. Some things we can consider doing include

Answering the phone when the secretary's busy or out

Pitching in on the playground patrol during recess

Maintaining the main bulletin board

Organizing a teacher appreciation day

Volunteering in the nurse's office

Compiling a school newsletter

Helping the librarian by offering
to handle story time once a month

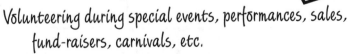

Volunteering during special events, performances, sales,
fund-raisers, carnivals, etc.

(One note of caution: It's one thing to have a desire to help, it's another to be annoyingly intrusive. The teacher, office staff, and librarian have schedules that our popping in "to help" can really disrupt. The best tactic is to arrange these efforts in advance.)

The Payoff

Our efforts to donate time, talents, and energy can yield much. They help us establish an attitude of partnership with the school and responsibility for its operation—whether through baking a cake for a fund-raiser or recruiting members for the parent-teacher organization. They can give us an inside track on the operation of the school, teacher personalities, routines, as well as a rare chance to see our kids in action at school—do they listen well? Are they eating dessert first and not having time to finish their sandwich? Do they cooperate on the playground? And finally, pitching in on campus helps us forge a relationship with the kids with whom our kids spend so much of their time.

3. Take Care of the # 1 Customer

We may be at the school every time the door is open, our child's teacher's best and most-dependable room mom, an active force in the parent-teacher organization, and we may know as much about our kids' daily routines as the teachers. But to leave our kids out of the loop means none of the above will do any good.
Following are ways we can help our students.

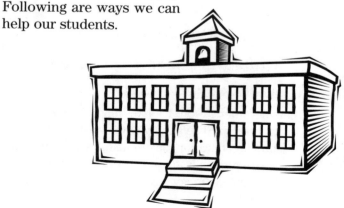

Establish good habits.

Set regular and reasonable homework times and bedtimes; equip a kid-friendly study center; and instill some cliched but tried-and-true principles such as "don't procrastinate," "do the worst first," and "break big jobs down into more manageable segments."

Teach good organizational skills.

Supply notebooks, purchase a student calendar or organizer, and post a large calendar to track upcoming due dates and tests. One mom uses different colored pens on a dry erase board to clearly designate scheduled field trips, tests, and appointments for each family member.

Read, read, read the information that comes home in the backpack each day.

It's a great habit to go through your child's backpack with a pen in one hand and the calendar nearby because these notes, memos, and announcements are usually chock-full of coming test dates, book report dates, teacher requests, permission slips, and tests to be signed.

Be available during homework time.

Help stumped kids; quiz kids who need to be quizzed; derail frustration; praise and prod your kids toward success.

Display and celebrate successes and victories.

Have an "I did it" bulletin board to show off good grades, ribbons, and special projects. Head for the ice cream shop to mark the meeting of a tough deadline or simply the survival of a rainy Monday when nothing seemed to go right.

Respect your kids.

There are fine lines between encouraging and nagging, between helping and doing, and between having high expectations and setting up stressful pressure.

Emphasize effort as well as achievement. Use failures as a challenge.

Ask, "How can we turn this around for the better?"

Be a security net.

Grades will tumble and failures will occur. Be there to "catch" your kids when they "fall." Then help them back up.

Teach study skills.

Show your kids how to make study sheets, note cards, diagrams, and summaries as well as how to use reference tools.

Pay attention to the little things.

We can do so much to make a difference in a school day. For example, halfway through the school year, Nick let on that he really likes his sandwiches cut on the diagonal because for some reason they're easier to eat. It sounds petty but we all have quirks like that. It's such a small way to make a hard day at school go a bit more smoothly.

Try some of these perky things too:

* Join the kids for lunch.

   Put a cheery note in your son's lunchbox.

   * Plaster your daughter's sandwich baggie with "You're #1" stickers.

   Occasionally send an extra-special snack.

* Take Popsicles to the whole class during recess on the first warm day of spring.

   Arrange a surprise bring-a-friend-home-after-school day.

From Field Trips to Recitals:
Don't Leave Home without It

As moms of preschoolers, we heard a lot about diaper-bag packing strategies, but it's just as important for moms of school-agers to learn how to properly pack a purse (or backpack or fanny pack). Whether we're en route to the dentist, in the bleachers at a soccer game, or on a school bus with 35 second graders heading for the museum, a well-stocked sack can be our greatest friend.

As anyone who saw the film *One Fine Day* knows, a thoroughly equipped purse such as the one Michelle Pfeiffer's character carried can do anything from feed a hungry first grader a nutritious breakfast to yield an impromptu superhero costume. So here goes. After picking the brains of fellow moms and slyly observing experienced grade-school teachers in action, here's a list of essentials for the handiest of handbags. (Hint: You'd better find a roomy one to hold all this stuff!)

- **Resealable bag or two** to hold the parts of a broken necklace, a pulled tooth, a soda-drenched hairbow
- **Permanent marker** for labeling drink boxes on field trips and putting names on craft projects at Scout meetings
- **Safety pins**—especially handy during recitals and programs that involve costumes
- **Self-stick notes and a pencil**
- **Calendar**
- **Small bottle of sunscreen**
- **Bobby pins**
- **Anti-bacterial gel**
- **Travel-size wet wipes** to clean messy hands, wipe off a grungy picnic table, or soothe playground scrapes
- **Tissues**
- **Bandages**
- **Snacks** from a pack of gum to a package of restaurant crackers, sometimes just having *something* to eat can save the day
- **Lip balm** to protect wind-chapped lips or to wax the string of a new yo-yo
- **Small scissors**
- **Nail file**
- **Rubber band**
- **Mending kit**
- **Money**—quarters are especially nice for the gum machine at the grocery store or the fish food dispenser at the zoo or at the baseball field where a coach needs a quarter to flip at the beginning of the game
- **Small toys**—small fast-food-meal trinkets can help kids pass time in lines and in the car

Sick Day Survival

"I don't feel very good." The vague complaint stops you in your tracks as you head toward the front door to make the morning run to school. "You don't feel warm," you say as you lay your hand across his forehead, noting that he does, now that he mentions it, look a little flushed. "It's not my head, it's my tummy." Quickly your mind races back through the past few meals he's eaten ... no red flags to indicate food poisoning. Could it be the stomach bug that's going around?

Now what to do, *what to do*? Take him on to school at the risk of getting a call in 30 minutes telling you he's running a fever of 103 degrees and—humiliation and misery of all humiliations and misery—just threw up in the classroom? Or keep him home for the mysterious malady, upsetting both of your schedules and the carpool routine for something which might turn out to be nothing more than a bubble of gas or a wave of multiplication test anxiety?

School "sick child" policies—which usually just tell parents to keep the child home when they're running a temperature, having diarrhea, breaking out with chicken pox, throwing up, or suffering through pink-eye—may not make it much easier for us to make the call on common symptoms such as a stomachache, a sore throat, a headache, or the "I don't feel so goods." We all know that you can be really sick without a temperature, so it usually takes more than a thermometer to help us decide.

"Ninety-nine percent of the time I follow my instincts as a mother, and 99 percent of the time my instincts are correct," says Susan, who usually doesn't find it too difficult to decide whether to keep her son, Jordan, a second grader, at home. "The one percent [of the time] I do not follow my instincts, they are usually right and I regret not doing so!"

Amanda, mother of four, says stressing the negative side of staying home sick usually helps her discern true illness from such afflictions as spring fever, the Monday morning blues, or a queasy bout of book report butterflies. "There have been times that my son says he has a stomach ache and I have let him stay home," she says. "But I am sure to tell him that he is not allowed to go outside, nor is he allowed to have any friends over after school gets out. He has to stay on the couch or in bed. That usually does the trick and he trots off to school, unless his stomach actually does hurt. I can usually tell if he is really sick; he gets very quiet and sits still, not like him at all!"

Caroline says when she has a child who's not feeling well in the morning, "usually I try to have my child ride with me in the car, as I take my [other] children to school. If, by the time we arrive at school, my child is still sick, I take him home with me." Keeping a close watch on her kids also helps her make those tough calls. "The best way to determine whether a child is actually ill is to watch him when he assumes you have lost interest or are preoccupied with breakfast or whatever. If the child is still listless and looks ill, he probably is truly ill."

Real or Fake?

Some of us have kids who just aren't built to be "fakers" because they love school and want to be there every day. "I do find it hard to make a call on a potential illness because my children take such pride in good attendance," says Janice, mom of two with one on the way. "If they promise to keep that tissue in their pocket or up their sleeve, then I tend to send them until it worsens. My two children, luckily, have such an enthusiasm and love for school and their teachers that I know for them to say they don't want to go to school, there has to be a problem," she says. "My oldest will even fight an illness where she absolutely has to stay home just to go to school. But basically, if they're appearing listless, tired, and are hard to get moving, if they have a certain redness in their cheeks with a slight to unusual cough or runny nose, then I know they're doomed for the day."

Other moms have kids they wouldn't put it past to, say, swish hot chocolate around in their mouths before they get their temperature taken. If that's the case at your house, here are some clues to help uncover the truth.

- Ask a few questions about the school day ahead. You may just find out that Mr. Dwinzel, the substitute teacher from the black lagoon, is supposed to fill in today, or that a certain homework paper due today isn't "exactly" done, or that the other kids have been leaving your child out of the reindeer games during recess. Those scenarios would drive any child to drastic action.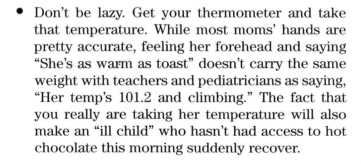

- Don't be lazy. Get your thermometer and take that temperature. While most moms' hands are pretty accurate, feeling her forehead and saying "She's as warm as toast" doesn't carry the same weight with teachers and pediatricians as saying, "Her temp's 101.2 and climbing." The fact that you really are taking her temperature will also make an "ill child" who hasn't had access to hot chocolate this morning suddenly recover.

- Recall whether you've heard about anything "going around" your school, church, or neighborhood. That might help you determine whether the case of the "itches" is more than a series of annoying mosquito bites.

- Give it the "lie down for 30 minutes" stalling technique. The truly sick child probably won't complain too much because he just feels too yucky. The bamboozler, on the other hand, will probably complain and find an excuse to pop up off the couch before five minutes are up.

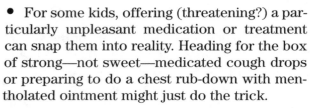

- For some kids, offering (threatening?) a particularly unpleasant medication or treatment can snap them into reality. Heading for the box of strong—not sweet—medicated cough drops or preparing to do a chest rub-down with mentholated ointment might just do the trick.

If your little loved one really is ill, it's time to kick some TLC into action:

- Keep a shelf in the kitchen stocked with Jell-O, Sprite, saltines, ready-to-freeze ice pops, and chicken noodle soup or broth.

- Set up the sick bed wherever your child feels the most comfortable. She may not want to be isolated back in her bedroom; if that's the case, pull out the hide-a-bed or make a pallet on the couch in the den.

- If it's an illness you know will be fairly long, or if your child's having to spend several days recuperating from surgery or an accident, make a grab bag of gifts. I still remember the bag of treats mom gave me when I came home from the hospital after my tonsillectomy. I opened one a day—they were trinkets like a new hairbrush, a book, and a new pair of pajamas. That gave me something to look forward to each day. Other great sack stuffers include the unopened kids' meal treats you've been stockpiling, leftover party favors, sketch pads, markers, a diary or journal, a mini photo album, activity books, a scrapbook, travel games, a CD or cassette, a video, a deck of cards, stationery, pajamas, house shoes, or slipper socks.

- Keep a sick-day activity kit stocked with crayons, markers, small toys, brain-teasers, activity books, stickers, etc., that you only pull out when illness strikes. Make a container for your collection out of a plastic-lidded box, a lap tray, a 13×9 cake pan, a shoebox, or even a bucket.

Whether we're walking with confidence or tripping clumsily over the speed bumps and around the curves that school days and all the decisions they encompass can throw onto our road, we can be sure of one thing: we have a Map—with a capital M—that can help us get and keep our bearings. It's the Bible and, if we check it regularly, we'll find that it not only can tell us where we should be going and how to get there, it also can alert us to danger signs, guide us safely through rough terrain, and point out the rest areas and scenic spots along the way. And through God's grace, we can get strength for the journey as well!

part III

The End Zone:
After School is Cool

chapter 5

Awesome Activities and Simple Pleasures:

Empowering Kids to Be All Content without the Additives

> "Even a child is known by his actions ..."
> —Proverbs 20:11

The season of school-age childhood includes two main parts: in-class time and out-of-school time. When school's out, a child's workday is only half over. How our kids spend their time out of school—an estimated 80 percent of their waking time in an average year—carries much more weight than we might imagine.

"A child's time out of school is the essential fabric of childhood and the underpinning of adult life," says author Joan Bergstrom in *School's Out, Now What?*[3] But this time, she says, "is an asset that can slip away like coins through a ripped pocket. Unstructured and unproductive use of this time can result in overexposure to television, overeating, fighting with siblings, hanging around, physical inertia, fear, loneliness, and withdrawal."[4]

If necessity is the mother of invention, then boredom must be the proud mom of having fun. Our world seems to have become so intent on throwing gizmos and gadgets, activities and lessons at our kids in order to prevent boredom during the out-of-school hours that fewer and fewer kids on the block are learning how to play—and love it—without all the additives.

There are many ways we can empower our kids to use their God-given imaginations and to be content without computer games, active without scheduled activities, and creative without classes. Here are some tips:

1. Let your yes be yes ...

... to the basics. A no-fail artillery includes much of the stuff that cluttered up our closets and garages when we were kids (note the absence of name-brand thingies that we frazzled parents may well have spent 12 hours tracking down this past Christmas!).

Things ...

to roll, toss, catch, and hit, and the things to whack them with, catch them with, and hit them over or into: baseball/bat/glove; Wiffle ball/bat; golf balls/clubs; tennis balls/rackets; badminton birdies/racquets/nets; basketball/hoop; football; soccer ball/goal

Tom Sawyer or Laura Ingalls likely played with: yo-yos, marbles, kites, tops, fishing poles

to build with such as blocks

to read: books, magazines

to ride (don't forget the helmet!): skateboard, bike, scooter, stilts (store-bought or hand-made from tin cans and rope), pogo stick, roller skates, in-line skates

to make things with: art supplies (see Chapter 6), model kits, paper (for paper airplanes and paper dolls, etc.)

to monkey around in or on: swing set, jungle gym, sandbox, tire swing, tree house, fort, playhouse to play pretend with: dress-up clothes, dolls and accessories, walkie talkies, "theme kits"—supplies for playing school, restaurant, beauty shop, rodeo, post office, etc.

to play with that are messy or wet: sandbox, water balloons, dirt pile, water sprinkler, wading pool, squirt and spray toys

to see things better with: flashlight, binoculars, telescope, magnifying glass

and a few other practical odds and ends: stopwatch, bug nets, jump rope, hula hoop, baton, board games (must haves include classics such as checkers and dominoes ... but be open to learning new ones together as well), puzzles, Silly Putty ... and the list goes on.

2. Let your no be no.

A well-placed *no* can fuel up a kid's think tank. A no—or at least a set of limits—regarding television can force a child off the couch and into the toy closet to find something to gainfully occupy his time. A no to some of the latest and greatest electronic games can take some of the polish off pushing buttons and propel a sluggish kid out the door to ride bikes. And a no to that one extra planned activity or lesson might free up time better spent just rattling around catching lightning bugs, making a cardboard box castle for a just-captured turtle, playing a newly invented game with the next-door neighbor. As unnatural as it may feel, saying no and leaving kids to their own devices is sometimes the only way we can help them discover for themselves the joy of "doing nothing."

3. Be spontaneous and flexible.

Try not to get into the "if it's not on my calendar it isn't considered" syndrome our crowded schedules too often force us into. If the kids want to have an impromptu supper in the fort they built, slice off some of that roast you've been cooking for four hours and let them have sandwiches in their new home. An attitude like this, in part, gives the kids a confidence-boosting sense of control over their environment ... and it just makes life fun.

4. Orchestrate variety.

Head home after school if your kids have had lots of planned activities going on after school for the past few days. Likewise, if you've been home a few days in a row after school, head for the park or ice cream shop one day. Encourage "solo" play when friends have been around so much that you sense nerves beginning to fray; invite friends over when you detect a need for socialization. Balance indoor play with outdoor play and creative "pretend" play (dress-up, etc.) with more cerebral "brain games" that call for problem solving or strategy.

5. Join the fun!

Just as helping in the classroom offers us a first-hand glimpse of our kids in action at school, becoming a player gives us a precious chance to see them in action come time for fun and games. I fall more in love with one friend each time I see her in action with our kids because if our girls are playing "hokey pokey" in dress-up clothes in the front yard, Tonya's "shaking it all around" right beside them. If the boys are tooling around with the chemistry set at the kitchen table, she's teaching them the scientific notation for oxygen as they go along. This mom doesn't wait for an invitation to enter their world; she knows she has a standing membership. Kids crave that kind of casual and playful interaction with parents. Moms who step up to the plate can score a home run of blessings—whether it's the opportunity to see a daughter share, to hear a son's rare belly laugh, to seize one of those rare "teachable moments," or simply to enjoy the fun and make memories.

6. Foster friendships.

 Watching my 7-year-old daughter and our 8-year-old next-door neighbor ride the roller coaster of little girl friendship is part of the drama of our home life these days. "Kelsey's my best friend in the world," Lindsey might lovingly proclaim one afternoon as she digs through her drawer to find a treasured trinket worthy of demonstrating her love for this little girl we prayed would move in next door. But just as quickly as the sky can darken before a summer storm, my little drama queen's countenance can instantaneously morph from love and adoration into scorn and spite. "I'm never playing with her ever again," she'll huff as she stomps down the hall sputtering a string of numerous but vague offenses. The cold war never lasts very long, though ... in just a few minutes she'll ask to use the phone to apologize to her friend, or she'll say she has to "run next door to get something I forgot."

As a "wise old mom" who realizes that if you have even one friend you can really count on in this world, you're blessed beyond measure, it's a bittersweet experience for me to witness firsthand the ups and downs of this tender friendship. Episodes like the one above dredge up both comforting memories of my own loyal childhood pals as well as disturbing memories of how astonishingly cruel playmates can be—a cutting remark, a missing birthday party invitation, a very intentional snub from a so-called "best" friend.

Despite the emotional risks, forming friendships is a key part of a child's school-age years. Friendships teach our kids about life and relationships, they provide a "non-relative" sounding board for our kids' ideas, they promote emotional and spiritual health and, perhaps best of all, they simply give our kids extra fun during both the in-school and out-of-school times.

As parents of school-age kids, it's up to us to coach our kids through these turbulent, friendship-forming years. We can walk the familiar "fine line" between helping and interfering when it comes to fostering friendships by

- Gently guiding them toward "desirable" friendships while giving them the freedom to make their own choices.
- Being their safety net when friendships fail.
- Tuning in to their friendship style. If they enjoy one-on-one relationships, don't push for big bashes come party time, and choose independent lessons and after-school activities (art lessons over Little League, for example). On the other hand, if they are social creatures who crave interaction with lots of kids, find ways for them to be involved in group projects and organizations.
- Spelling out some of the good rules of friendship. Just because we've grown up knowing that we should treat others as we want to be treated, we can't assume our kids will know how to apply this to their friendships. They need to be told. And told. And told.

- Listening and watching. In this day and age, tragically, we can't assume that the kids our kids are around in the neighborhood and on the school playground come from families with a similar set of values and expectations as ours. Some might call this spying or manipulation, but the stakes are higher than ever before and we can't afford to take anything for granted. Tuning in to the conversations and actions of our kids and their friends can help us spot any red flags and head off danger before it has a chance to get a foothold in the lives of our little ones.

Stuff to Do
WHEN THERE'S
NOTHING TO DO

In keeping with the spirit of *Celebrate Home*, which offered busy moms of preschoolers a list of tried-and-true activities for those "I'm bored" moments, here's another list of things to do gathered by an idea-hungry mom who always needs ideas to suggest when the school-age set complains, "But there's nothing to do, Mom!"

Interestingly, when asked to name their kids' favorite activities, the majority of moms surveyed listed what would be considered "simple pleasures" fueled by imagination or body power; in other words, "No batteries required!"

Outside

Whether you have country acres, an apartment terrace, a suburban backyard, or a nearby city park, head outdoors for the following kinds of fun:

✔ Ride bikes

✉ Sketch nature drawings

————————— ✱ Play in the water

————————————— ✘ Shoot some hoops

★ Jump on a trampoline

————————— ☞ Play catch

————————————— ✔ Swing

★ Do tricks on the monkey bars

————————— ☞ Practice gymnastic tricks

✘ Plant a tree, flower, or vegetable garden

✱ Collect rocks

✔ Build a bird feeder and start a bird-watching station

————————————— ✱ Play hide-and-seek

☞ Organize a game of kick-the-can

✘ Draw a themed mural on the sidewalk, driveway, or patio

————————— ★ Jump into a game of hopscotch

————————————— ☞ Sand sculpt

✔ Build a snowman

————————— ★ Throw some horseshoes

————————————— ✉ Learn how to grass whistle

✔ Wash the car, bikes, lawn furniture, outdoor toys

★ Jump rope (check out a book from the library that lists some new chants to learn)

————————— ✱ Build a fort

✘ Have an Easter egg hunt (if it's fall, have a pine cone hunt; if it's summertime, paint some rocks and have a rock hunt)

★ Wash the dog

✉ Hang a hula hoop from a tree branch; take turns having water balloon tossing practice

————————— ✱ Play badminton

★ Dress up the dog

   ☞ Hold a talent show on the patio or deck

✔ Celebrate a coming holiday with a bike parade

✆ Do messy art projects (see Chapter 6 for ideas)

   ✳ Set up a tent and camp out

————— ☞ Make mud pies

————————— ✘ Stage a circus

★ Round up a Wiffle ball team for an evening tournament

   ☞ Find some critters—bugs, frogs, lizards

————— ✳ Ride skateboards

✔ Be a scientist: use a magnifying glass out to seek out and collect samples of natural matter to examine under a microscope

   ✳ View the nighttime sky with a telescope

————— ★ Build a balance beam

————————— ☞ Play Frisbee

✘ Find a nearby creek or stream and look for fish, tadpoles, crawdads, turtles

★ Set up an obstacle course using odds and ends from the garage—jump through tires, crawl through hoops, scoot in boxes, rake a ball to the finish line

✔ Build, sand, and paint something from wood scraps, pine cones, fallen tree limbs

   ★ Set up a lemonade stand

————— ✆ Find a comfy, shady spot to curl up and read a book

————————— ✘ Go on a scavenger hunt

✳ Find a grassy slope to roll down or slide down on a box lid

————— ☞ Make wildflower garlands

————————— ★ Hunt for four-leaf clovers

Inside

Whether the weather has locked you in or whether you just feel like hanging around inside, try some of the following for indoor fun:

✔ Have a board game tournament

☞ Play hide-and-seek or sardines

★ Play cards—revive old favorites like "Crazy Eight" and "Go Fish" that are good for any age

————— ✳ Build card houses

————————— ☞ Play charades

✆ Look through old photos

————— ✔ Make brown-paper-sack costumes: a cowboy vest, a hula skirt, etc.

✳ Roll out butcher paper and design a mural the length of your longest hallway

✗ Build a box-and-construction-paper village

————— ☞ Create a private hideout in a closet

☞ Play dress-up, grocery store, restaurant, singer, etc.

✗ Set up a beauty shop/nail salon for "makeovers"

✔ Dig into the arts and crafts box or closet

★ Bake something

————— ✗ Update your scrapbook

————————— ☞ Sew something

————— ✆ Start or write in a diary

✳ Play that "the floor is a crocodile-infested swamp" and make your way through it by tossing down cardboard "stepping stones"

✔ Have a taste test (take turns offering a variety of tasty samples to a blindfolded player; see how many she guesses correctly. Some to try: pickle juice, Kool-Aid, peanut butter, water, marshmallow cream, chocolate syrup, a dash of salt. Use the small bathroom-sized paper cups to offer samples.)

★ Start a great big jigsaw puzzle on a card table or the dining room table

✗ Set up an obstacle course in the living room

✔ Hang a hula hoop or smaller ring from a doorway and hold a paper airplane building and flying contest

———— ☞ Write a book

———— ✏ Play with the chemistry set

✳ Design and draw a maze for a friend to solve

✏ Mix concoctions from whatever ingredients Mom will let you have in the kitchen

———— ★ Write and stage a puppet show

✳ Construct a marshmallow and toothpick tower

☞ Set up a perfumery/scent factory at the bathroom counter. Mix and match drops of good-smelling lotions and potions; soak cotton balls in them to make sachets

———— ✔ Work puzzles in an activity book—mazes, word scrambles, etc.

✏ Make a foil sculpture—make 3-D art or costumes from foil

———— ★ Design/invent your own board game

———— ☞ Make a rubber band ball

✗ Sort through and organize your collections: get a scrapbook for those stamps you've been accumulating; make a divided box lid into a display case for your rocks.

✔ Decorate and hang a bulletin board in your room. Tack up snapshots, Bible verses, reminders, party invitations, etc.

———— ✳ Listen to music; choreograph a dance to it or write your own lyrics

———— ✗ Read a good book

chapter 6

Art Smart:
Teach Your Kids to Be Creative Even If You Don't Think You Are!

> "Lift your eyes and look to the heavens: Who created all these? He who brings out the starry host one by one, and calls them each by name."
> —*Isaiah 40:26*

What a creative God, our Creator God, who "*sits enthroned above the circle of the earth and ... stretches out the heavens like a canopy*" (Isaiah 40:22)! Made in His image, we can draw from the limitless well of creativity He has equipped us with time after time ... to serve Him, to serve others, and simply to enjoy the life He's given us through His Son, Jesus.

Creativity Counts

Creativity unlocks the doors of a child's imagination and lifts the lid off apparent limitations. Creative kids say, "I can," instead of "I can't"; they find something to do when the power goes out or when they're waiting their turn in a dentist's office. They seldom complain of boredom and often have healthy levels of self-confidence. Creative kids aren't as quickly frustrated in the face of challenge or new situations and they see potential and possibilities where others see dead ends and brick walls.

It's a Way of Life

Parents can nurture creativity in the home by making it a way of life, so to speak. Here are some ideas to help you enhance your kids' creativity.

Show them your own creativity in action.

Let them see you and others in your family being creative. "But I'm not creative at all!" you complain. Creativity isn't limited to drawing, painting, or composing music. You're creative if you bake, garden, work with needy families, cook, wrap gifts, decorate your home, cut hair, teach Sunday school ... the list goes on.

Let your kids see you doing it, let them know what you enjoy about doing it, and let them in on some of the process you're going through while you do it: "I have to decide what color to use here. If I use this red against that brown, it might not show up. But apples are red. This is going to take some figuring out. What do you think?"

Let your son hang around Grandma's house when you know she has a quilting project in the works. Send your daughter outside to help Dad put in the springtime flowerbeds. Bring the kids into the action when you're trying to come up with a new dish for dinner.

Show them you value creativity.

Be ecstatic over what they've made. Let them see you watching them and admiring their creative process. Spend money on things that are creative. If I had only $2.00 left to my name, I'd rather spend it on a book than on food. Adopt that attitude about creative tools—let the kids know it's usually money well spent to visit a museum, buy a drawing tablet, pick up a new CD.

Make frequent visits to museums, concerts, plays, art shows. Point out the creativity of others in the world. A Discovery Channel program detailing the history of space travel gave a captivated Nick a vivid picture of the reality (and frequency) of failure as well as the glory and satisfaction of success. Don't underestimate a child's ability to appreciate fine art, classical music, timeless dramas. Take them to *Annie*, sure; but don't be afraid to take them to see your favorite opera too.

Use your purchasing power to prejudice your kids toward creative play.

When you're spending money on or for the kids, buy games and toys that are imagination-fueled, that power up their problem-solving skills, that require building or strategizing. Guide them to invent their own games at home. Facilitate their efforts when they want to build sheet-and-chair forts, play dress-up, or put on a puppet show. Make yourself handy so you can help them over hurdles. "The sheet won't stay over the chair!" the little fort-builders cry, ready to give up. Resist the urge to carry them over that hurdle by taking over and fixing it for them. Simply hand them some clothespins or safety pins and innocently say, "I wonder if these might help somehow ..."

Raise them to be readers.

This territory has been well-traveled; just remember that reading can inspire, instruct, equip, and entertain the creative mind. (Deirdre homeschools her five kids. They have to take a laundry basket to the library to carry all their books. At first, the librarian was suspicious and figured they didn't really read all those books each week. Now she knows better.)

Let them see you put their creativity in action.

Don't re-do the less-than-neat gift wrapping job your son did on his grandma's birthday present. Let him know you appreciate his help, what a nice job he did, and how much time he saved you. After losing her eyeglass case last fall, Lindsey folded some construction paper into an envelope-like replacement. I'm sure it didn't protect the lenses as it should—but for the day or two that she used her creation before we found the original, she felt pleased to have come up with a solution to her problem.

Kick-Start Art at Home

The classroom or an art studio isn't the only place for your kids to launch their creativity. In fact, sadly enough, many schools don't spend much time at all on creative endeavors. Give young artists a head start right in your own home—even if you don't have a creative bone in your body! All you do is provide the tools, the space, and a few ideas ... your kids will take care of the rest.

The Tools

You don't need to spend a fortune on a fancy art kit from a hobby or art store—and avoid buying only coloring/activity books that limit a child's opportunity to exercise her imagination. Supplement these supplies with activities/books that allow her to put her own ideas into action such as the *My More-than-Coloring Books* series from Concordia (1999). Spend your time at these places to keep your art nook well stocked:

✔ **discount centers**   ✔ **junk stores**

✔ **dollar stores**   ✔ **flea markets**

✔ **fabric stores**

✔ **office supply centers**

Also, let friends and family members know you're interested in having any usable, discarded business products they may run across in their jobs. Your bounty may include boxes, scrap printer paper, packing materials, and more. As you gather supplies, keep in mind that you'll need the following materials as well.

Materials to Mark On

- ✔ White paper for sketching and drawing—a box of computer paper is usually a penny-wise investment, and you can also purchase inexpensive newsprint. Check with your local newspaper to see if you can buy their unprinted end-rolls.
- ✔ Heavyweight stock for painting—store-bought paint pads, brown mailing paper, and butcher paper work well. Also save all the heavyweight white or brown paper sacks you get when you buy from certain department stores—the unprinted side makes a great painting sheet.
- ✔ Colored tissue paper
- ✔ A rainbow assortment of construction paper

Materials to Mark With

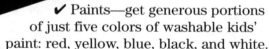

- ✔ Pencils—both # 2 and colored pencils
- ✔ Washable markers— angled tips serve double-duty by allowing artists to draw with either fine or fat lines
- ✔ Crayons

- ✔ Paints—get generous portions of just five colors of washable kids' paint: red, yellow, blue, black, and white. If you don't know basic color mixing, now's the time to learn. Get online or pull out the encyclopedia for a quick rundown and make learning about colors your first project together. Offer older kids a variety of paints—watercolors and acrylics, for starters.

✔ Paint brushes—round up chunky ones for the younger kids, a more varied assortment for older artists.

Materials to Put Things Together With

✔ Glue—again, gather an assortment. Don't ever be without washable school glue, but also offer access to rubber cement, fabric glue, paste, wood glue, etc., each of which has a more specific purpose.

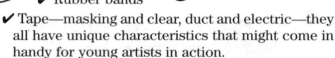

✔ Stapler
✔ Clothes pins
✔ Paper clips
✔ Brads
✔ Rubber bands

✔ Tape—masking and clear, duct and electric—they all have unique characteristics that might come in handy for young artists in action.

Three-Dimensional Materials

✔ Glitter
✔ Paper sacks—both grocery-sized and lunch-sized, both white and brown, for puppets, backpacks, treasure maps, scavenger hunts, and more.
✔ Empty boxes and containers
✔ Cotton balls
✔ Cotton-tipped swabs
✔ Yarn—assorted colors and weights
✔ String
✔ Buttons
✔ Lids
✔ Cardboard tubes
✔ Wrapping paper scraps
✔ Old greeting cards
✔ Wood scraps

- ✔ Rubber bands
- ✔ Coffee filters
- ✔ Paper plates
- ✔ Styrofoam plates
- ✔ Sand
- ✔ Clay
- ✔ And don't forget the scissors. Now you've armed your child with the stuff that imaginations are made for!

The Space

Most parents cite the mess as their number one reason for not nurturing their kids' creativity at home. They simply don't relish the thought of their young Picasso slinging paint on the country French breakfast table or dribbling blue on the carpet. But you can prevent practically any artistic mess that might arise with a little planning and a couple of inexpensive vinyl tablecloths.

First, consider the most practical spot in your home to set up your junior artist. The kitchen? That's often a great choice because of the usually easy-to-clean table and floors. Besides, moms often can snatch a couple of minutes to do some kitchen chores while the kids are immersed in their projects. But think before you park the kids here. Is it nearly dinnertime? Will you have to cut the art session short to set the table? What about the bathroom? (It's not *that* silly if you happen to have a roomy, easy-to-wipe-off counter. The bathroom has a

> I like my mom being at home… because I like that we get to see her all the time. I'm glad… we don't have to go to day care and she can play with us.
>
> —Lauren, age 5

handy supply of water and usually plenty of light.) A bedroom? Sometimes spreading out on the floor beats sitting at a table. Garage or carport? (Especially for bulky projects.) Wherever you decide, make sure it's an uncluttered spot with plenty of light and ample elbow room at the actual work surface. It doesn't have to be an area with space to store your supplies. Stow those in totable containers such as baskets, tool boxes, school boxes, resealable bags, and oversized under-bed storage bins. Stash paints and brushes in giant coffee cans under the kitchen or bathroom sink where kids will be rinsing brushes and washing their hands after their artistic endeavors.

Once you've decided where to situate the imagination station, prevent messes by protecting work surfaces. You may automatically run for the newspapers, but they're not always the best because the ink rubs off on elbows and on the surface below. Vinyl tablecloths are a better first line of defense. Spread them underfoot to protect carpet and flooring, and cover your tabletop to protect wood surfaces from paint drips and scissors scratches. For an instant easel, tack a vinyl tablecloth to the wall and simply use masking tape to affix the paper to the work surface. Dad's old shirts are classic paint smocks, or you can buy cute ones at hobby shops. Or if you're handy at sewing, craft a useful art smock from one of those vinyl tablecloths. Another tip I recently learned: Have the kids wear their painting garb inside out.

Artists need to develop neat habits early on—let them know that cleanup and proper care of equipment are as much a part of "doing art" as the project itself. Make neatness convenient: Pack the paint shirt, apron or smock, a spray bottle of water, and a roll of paper towels with the art gear. The motto "clean as you go" helps youngsters remember to swab up paint globs and sweep up glitter overflow before the mess gets out of hand.

A Few Ideas

If you are a parent who, as a student,
opted for choir, band, athletics, chemistry—
anything besides art; and if you, even
now, cringe when your child hands you
a blank piece of paper and commands,
"Draw a horse, Mom," these ideas
might spark your imagination so you
can ignite your child's creativity
at home.

Keep an idea file or notebook. Clip and file art activities detailed in magazines. Take how-to notes during the art segments of children's programming. Tap into online resources. That way, you're not stymied by having to come up with an idea from scratch when your kid announces, "I want to make something." Just pull a fun idea out of your hat—or your file box.

"I bet you can make one even better than that." The next time your child sees a toy commercial and starts in with the "I want its," fan that spark of desire into a flaming creative challenge by saying, "I bet you can make one even better than that." A few boxes, some fabric scraps, the scissors, tape, and glue will start to become your daughter's fashion-doll dream house before the jingle on the commercial begins to fade away. A garbage bag and some twine convert your son's action figure into a parachuting paratrooper; a paper grocery sack becomes a super-deluxe backpack; and some toilet paper tubes and a giant foil ball become a game of bowling. You don't have to come up with the technical details—just provide the tools and the idea and your child will take them and run!

Hit the books. Use books as a springboard for creativity. Find arty ideas in favorite storybooks. Make tin-can telephones a la the Berenstain Bears in *No Girls Allowed*. Invent and draw or sculpt a menu item even more outrageous than green eggs and ham. Trace the shape of a fairy tale character and ask your child to put a face on each one expressing different emotions. "Make the character look sad," "Make the character look surprised," etc.

Think simple and abstract. Use materials in their purest forms and for the most basic of designs. Instead of suggesting the intimidating, "Draw Grandpa's farm," provide one or two colors of construction paper for a torn-paper rendition of a single object the child might find on Grandpa's farm: an apple, a sheep, a barn, a tractor. Create wild and wacky critters from a glob of paint dropped onto a thick white sheet of paper. Play with patterns and designs by notching the sides of crayons or taping together a cluster of markers.

Shift the point of view. Play a game called "look up, look down." Tell your child he is standing under a tree in a park. The season is fall. Tell him to look up, and draw (or paint, or color) what he sees. Then tell him to look down, and do the same. Use other themes such as the beach, fire station, grocery store, Grandma's house, airport, etc. Variations on this imagination-stretching exercise are limitless, and you're sure to love the results.

As you guide your children through their artistic endeavors, keep the following in mind:

> **Respect the outcome.** Too many children—even without our help—develop a "perfection complex" about their artwork. They get nervous when it's not perfect and they want to keep starting over until they "get it right." When the results of an endeavor aren't what you or your child expect, don't fret, and by all means, don't jump in

with your eraser or correcting fluid to try to "fix" it. Rejoice! Say, "That's even neater than we had hoped it would be!" Or, "Look at what a happy turn of events that was ... that paint drip looks like a beautiful flower!"

On the other hand, don't hand your child one or two sheets of paper and expect her to turn out a masterpiece on one of her allotted rations. That's why you scouted out inexpensive paper sources. Professional artists go through sketch after sketch until they get the desired effect. If your child really doesn't like the way his first couple attempts turn out, say, "No big deal! Use this newsprint to keep trying until you get it just the way you want it."

Leave your suggestions and assignments open-ended. The kind of skill needed to produce a specific desired outcome takes years of advanced art training to learn. Expecting specific results ("a sunset over the river that looks just like the one on that postcard") only sets young artists up for certain failure.

Point out the difference between photographs and drawings. That may seem obvious, but a child can't always tell the difference. He might pick a photo in a magazine to try to draw, then try as he might he can't get his image to look like the one he's attempting to copy.

Don't be alarmed if the kids get stuck in a groove. Nick, after three years of drawing, painting, building, and sculpting the Titanic every which way that big old boat could be drawn, painted, built, and sculpted, has just now moved on to drawing cartoon characters and animals. If your daughter only uses houses as the subject of her artwork or your son sticks to racecars as his main focus, just let it go. Getting good at one subject gives kids confidence. They learn more than we realize as they study and present their favorite subjects in a variety of mediums. Always be ready to encourage them to venture on to other horizons, though!

Invest in art lessons. If you are considering investing in your child's creativity through art lessons, look for a teacher with a kid-friendly personality who not only teaches the mechanics of design, but who emphasizes the creative process as well. Your best bet, especially during the introductory years, is to choose a course that offers experiences in a variety of projects rather than in one specialized medium such as pen and ink. Steer clear of teachers or studios with a big push on competitions, especially in the early years.

Grab a paintbrush and join in the fun! For right here, right now, your job as "teeny league" art coach requires you simply to grant your child access to a variety of materials, give her a comfortable place to work, and react to her efforts in a way that gives her the confidence to keep taking creative leaps. The kids love it when we work alongside them ... but tune in to their needs. If you sense that they are spending too much time bragging on your more advanced efforts and comparing their results to yours, you might want to find something else to do for a while. Give them some space to concentrate on their efforts but stay close enough to offer encouragement and guidance, and to steer them from frustrating circumstances into satisfying results.

Learn something new together. What fun to learn a new craft or technique together! Pick something you've never done—papier-mâché, candle making, beading—the kids will enjoy seeing Mom struggle a bit to figure out the instructions, and you will be amazed at the help they can offer you. They think grown-ups know everything ... this will help teach them the valuable lesson that you're never too old to learn something new!

Give your kids the latitude simply not to like doing something. You might get all pumped up about making a tissue-paper Easter egg similar to the ones you enjoyed making in Sunday school as a child, but you find after gathering all the materials and parking at the table together that your daughter doesn't like to get her hands that messy. So there you are, finishing up two sticky eggs while she's drifted off to delve into the Lego bucket. Try to let it slide. Kids, like us, have natural preferences and aversions. Some prefer drawing to crafting, others enjoy making 3-D creations more than painting. The key: offer exposure to a variety of activities so they can explore each medium and method on their own.

25 Simple Art Activities
(So You Don't Have to Think of Them)

The following simple activities and exercises will keep you from having to stop and think when the kids say, "I wanna make something" or when they're staring blankly at a "RugRats" rerun and you think they could really be doing something more creative with their time. The ideas aren't arranged in any particular order; keep in mind the age and stage of your kids when choosing the activity you want to suggest. Remember, however, that sometimes age doesn't have that much to do with it—my son has been handling a stapler since he was 3 simply because I know he's a careful, cautious child. On the other hand, I know some 10-year-olds I still wouldn't trust with a stapler unless I was hovering over their shoulder!

Most of these ideas are included based on their simplicity, because busy moms find it easier to say no or to find excuses to put off art time when lots of preparation or expense is involved. A hint: Go through the list with a stack of note cards in hand. Jot down the ideas you like (that are age- and stage-appropriate for your kids) and start your own card file of imagination-starters. Then you take over from there—next time you're flipping through a parenting magazine that offers ideas or instructions for a project you think the kids would like, clip and paste or jot them onto other note cards to add to your growing collection. As you add each new idea to your file, make a separate supply list for your purse so you'll remember to pick them up when you're out and about.

1. Paper Dolls

You need: tracing paper, cardboard, colored pencils or crayons, scissors, paper clips

Trace a full-shot picture of your favorite story-book character, then transfer the tracing to a piece of heavy cardboard. Cut out and then design new clothes for him or her. Attach to your new paper doll with paper clips. Older kids can turn this into a history lesson by tracing a character from a history book and dressing the doll with the appropriate fashions of the day.

2. Shaving Cream Dreams

You need: shaving cream, muffin tin, toothpicks, food color, paper or cookie sheet

Put a dollop of shaving cream into each compartment of a muffin tin. Tint with food color (stir with toothpicks) and enjoy your fresh-smelling finger paints. Experiment by mixing colors.

3. You Finish the Picture

You need: stickers or magazine photos of faces; paper, pencil

Cut stickers or magazine photos in half and stick or glue to a sheet of white paper. On one sheet, try to match your drawing as closely as you can to the image; on another, make the completed image as silly as you can.

4. Color Fun

You need: old, broken crayons, baby food jars, candy molds

Peel paper from old, broken crayons and sort pieces by color families into baby food jars (these are good jobs for younger siblings who want in on the action). Melt the crayon bits in a double-boiler and pour into lightly oiled candy molds. When set, have fun with your newly recycled crayons! A great kid-to-kid gift.

5. Marble Maze

You need: cardboard tubes, masking tape, marbles, scissors

Create a chute system for your marbles by taping together cardboard tubes. Can you build a structure that will transport a marble from your bed to your desk? From your desk to the floor?

6. Scavenger Hunt

Have someone give you a list of nature items to scout out in your yard or at the park (pine cones, acorns, sticks, rocks, grass). Bring them inside and let them inspire you. A heart-shaped rock? Paint it into a Valentine! A feathery piece of grass? Use it for a paintbrush! Let your imagination take off!

7. Play Clay Zoo

You need: play clay, odds and ends from your art box

Make play clay with your mom or dad, then shape globs into your favorite zoo animals. You don't have to stick to clay—put toothpick spines onto the porcupine's back, a cotton tail on the bunny, feathers on the peacocks.

8. Scrunch 'n' Tape

You need: scrap paper, masking tape

Use crumpled newspaper, newsprint, junk mail, or magazine pages to create 3-D forms. Can you form an animal? A fruit? A family?

9. Artists in Action

Go to the library and check out a book on a famous artist whose work you like. Look at the way he or she draws or paints, and see if you can imitate that technique to draw or paint your own project.

10. Filter Fun

You need: coffee filters, watercolors, brushes, pipe cleaners

Dab watercolor paints into designs onto a coffee filter. Wrap a pipe cleaner around the center and watch a beautiful butterfly come to life! Use another pipe cleaner to fashion antennae.

11. Line Art

You need: Paper and pencil

See what objects you can draw without lifting your pencil from the page.

12. Making Books

You need: paper, pencils/markers/crayons, stapler or hole punch, ribbon

Tell a story with pictures and print (or have your mom or dad print) the words that go under each picture. Bind sheets with stapler or hole punch and ribbon. Share your book with a friend!

13. Marshmallow Mountain

You need: large marshmallows, toothpicks

Use toothpicks and marshmallows to build a mountain or a tower. See how tall you can get it. Figure out ways to make the construction stronger.

14. My Town

You need: a piece of poster board or a large sheet of paper, crayons, markers

Pretend you're in an airplane flying over your neighborhood or town. Draw what you see. Where's the store, the church, Grandma's house?

15. Colorful Creatures

You need: thick paint, heavyweight paper

Fold a sheet of paper in half. Drop some colorful globs of paint into the crease and fold again. Open the paper. Let the image dry and see what details you can add to your creature to make it come alive.

16. Craft Stick Critters

You need: glue, markers, craft sticks

Use craft sticks to construct characters from one of your favorite storybooks. Act out the story for friends. Make up your own ending.

17. Junk Mail Jubilee

You need: a collection of junk mail, scissors, tape or glue, paper

Cut or tear junk mail into irregularly shaped pieces. Glue those pieces into a design for a new stamp.

18. Wonka Vision

You need: paper, crayons or markers

Name and describe a new treat manufactured by Willie Wonka's candy factory. Design and draw or color the wrapper.

19. Snow Scene

You need: black or navy construction paper, white chalk, hairspray

Draw a snowy scene with chalk on the sheet of dark paper. To preserve the picture and keep it from smudging, finish it off with a coat of hairspray.

20. Tire Tracks

You need: an old Matchbox or Hot Wheels car, paint, thick paper, marker

Dip the car's wheels in your paint and see where the tracks take you! Make designs from the tire tracks. Or make a road map with the tracks, then draw in landmarks with a marker.

21. Wacky Critters

You need: clothespins, scissors, felt scraps, glue, rubber bands

What wacky critters can you create using these materials? Create a critter or two, then make up a story about them. Get a friend to help you act it out.

22. Dots and Spots

You need: paper and crayons or markers

Compose an entire picture out of nothing but dots and spots. No lines allowed! How do you make certain areas darker without coloring them in? How can you make certain objects look rough? Shiny?

23. Etching

You need: crayons, paper, India ink, toothpicks

Completely cover a page with lots of areas of color (bear down hard when coloring). Don't leave any white spots. Paint over crayon page with India ink. Keep adding coats until it's well covered. Once it's dry, use a toothpick to etch a colorful springtime scene.

24. Craft Stick Construction

You need: craft sticks, glue

Use the craft sticks to build a log cabin, a super-tall building, or a bridge. Check out some books about architecture to get other ideas.

25. Drawing between the Lines

You need: sketch pad, pencils

This is a great exercise for serious artists in training. Set up a "still life" (a collection of objects you arrange in a pleasing way to look at while you draw). Bottles, fruit, vases, books, balls, shoes, tennis racket—anything's fair game if it's something you'd like to draw. First, draw what you see. Next, look at the "negative spaces." (That's what artists call the space in between the objects.) Draw the shapes of the "negative spaces" you see. Now draw the objects again. Sometimes studying the "negative space" can help you figure out a better way to draw the objects.

Art Gallery

If you have a prolific artist in residence, what can you do with all those creations? Here are some ideas gathered from moms and teachers through the years:

Designate a certain spot to be the art gallery: sticky-tack paintings and drawings on a bedroom or closet door, or the laundry room wall.

Buy a special bulletin board to display work.

Rely on that trusty old stand-by, the refrigerator.

Clear a bookshelf or the kitchen windowsill to make room to display 3-D projects that can't be hung.

Buy a scrapbook (or a photo album with magnetic pages) for your child to turn into a portfolio of her best work.

Have your child decorate pizza boxes—they make sturdy and stackable storage containers for artwork.

Thrill your child by having a piece or two of his collection matted and framed, and displaying your selections in a prominent spot in your home.

Share artwork with family and friends by turning it into gift wrap, greeting cards, or placemats (press between two sheets of clear self-adhesive shelf paper). Transfer snazzy kidprints onto T-shirts, aprons, and canvas tote bags using fabric paint, beads, or sequins.

Give a project a set "shelf-life" to be on display; after that, take a photo of it to paste in an art scrapbook and toss the original.

Remember—_always_ put your child's name and the date on the projects you keep. You may think you'll never forget the day when your first grader hands you her latest self-portrait ... but three birthdays, five lost teeth, and six best friends from now, your memory might not be so vivid.

chapter 7

"Taking" Things:
Avoiding Overcommitment

> "Be shepherds of God's flock that is under your care."
> —*I Peter 5:2*

We're all familiar with the stereotypical "hurried" kid, whose typical afternoon and evening include changing from school clothes to a gymnastics leotard in the back seat of the car as Mom scouts out the nearest fast-food place to pick up an energy-boosting snack of fries and a Coke between stops. After gymnastics, it's over to a friend's house to ride together to art lessons, and only after that does the pooped 8-year-old get to come home, kick off her shoes, and wiggle her bare toes in the carpet before plopping on the couch for some downtime with her favorite show, "The Brady Bunch." But wait! "Get into your uniform! You've got a game tonight," Mom's shouting to her brother, that hysterical edge in her voice as she's digging through the laundry hamper to find the socks that she hasn't had time to wash since the last game. The girl and her brother grab tacos from the take-out sack sitting on the breakfast bar, and shovel them down as they jump into the back seat.

This snapshot of childhood isn't one any of us would want to paste into our kids' memory books. But at least parts of this scenario are all too familiar in many of our own homes. When the kids hit grade school, it seems, the opportunities for lessons and organized extracurricular activities start knocking at our door, and like the battery bunny, they just keep on knocking, and knocking, and knocking. We begin to feel more like chauffeurs than shepherds.

It's easy to let our kids' involvement snowball because really, there's nothing "wrong" with lessons and activities. In fact, there's a lot "right" about them that benefits any child of God. For example, "They provide good learning experiences and build confidence," notes DeAnn, mom of two. This kind of activity also can help kids tap into their God-given talents and strengths.

"I want to expose [my son] to a variety of things so he can decide what he really likes, and hopefully narrow down the field," explains Gina.

Tula says this is her motive for allowing her kids to participate in organized activities as well. "We have tried to discover each child's special gifts and point them in that direction," she says. "For example, my oldest daughter excels in drama so we have her in piano and drama activities at church. My middle child is extremely gifted in dance, so she works with a young lady in our church 30 minutes a week. My son is very athletic. He plays baseball in the summer and basketball in the fall."

Participation in sports and activities also offers much-needed physical activity in this sedentary society. As soccer coach of Lindsey's pony-tailed team, Kurt says he's noticed a big improvement in the physical stamina of each girl as the weeks have gone by. At the beginning of the season, they were huffing and puffing, limping and complaining after just a few minutes of practice; now, a month and a half later, they have a bounce in their step almost to the end of practice.

Organized activities and sports also can offer important lessons about self-discipline and dependability, teamwork and cooperation, and they can place kids in a new circle of friends with the same interests. "Since my kids are home-schooled, they need the contact with other children," notes Mary, mom of two.

So with all these "plusses," how do we go wrong when we sign the permission slip for tae kwon do, piano lessons, or the bike club? It boils down to one word: overcommitment. Moms who "have it all together" stress that this is something they must consciously avoid.

"There are just not enough hours in the day to accomplish all that needs to be done, much less all we want to do," says Gina. "Even Bradley has expressed frustration over not enough time to just be together as a family and do nothing! So for sanity—not to mention financial drain—we do limit our activities." Right now, she says, what's working for Bradley is involvement in Boy Scouts and one sport per season, except during summer, which "we leave open for family activities."

66 I worked when my kids were babies, but have since come home to work and felt like the time was right now that they are in school— for lots of reasons. They are so busy! They are in piano and dance, T-ball and swimming. I felt so guilty not being the one to be at their events, etc., to support them, get them there, help with their anxieties, deal with a forgotten ball glove, etc. They have needs that are very different now that they are in school: making friends, making choices, homework. I miss working, but feel very blessed to be here— especially when they walk in the door after school. I am the first person they see and the first person they tell about their day. 99

—Louise, mother of two

Jane, mom of two teens, combats overcommitment by paying attention to when the activities take place. "We do not do something every day because it is important to be at home and be with family," she says. "Too many activities do not let the kids enjoy being home."

When considering what to let your kids join:

1. Give serious thought to why you're giving this activity serious thought. "Everything is so competitive," says author and mom Sharon Hoffman. "Kids are being forced to grow up and forced to mature so quickly, and they're put into that hectic pace so quickly that they're not even having a childhood. We need to live as if, 'Is this going to matter two years from now?' or 'Is this going to matter in light of eternity?' "

   Does the activity you're considering reflect a real passion of your child or does it represent your own wishes for your child? Just because you grew up on the softball field doesn't mean your daughter will be as well suited for the sport. She may prefer canvas and paintbrush to cleats and pop flies.

2. Make sure the activity fits and/or enhances your child's personality. Some kids prefer the independence of sports and activities such as tennis and art, while others thrive on the teamwork and interaction of ball teams and service organizations. Some kids seem to embrace and enjoy competition; others shy away from competitive activity, instead deriving their best dose of confidence from personal achievements such as a completed painting or an expertise in rock collecting.

3. Make sure your child is ready for the commitment. Just because organized sports and lessons are offered in your community for kids as young as 3, don't rush them into anything. Starting a 4-

year-old in T-ball when his stage of development tells you he'd rather watch bugs in the grass than field grounders is only likely to cause "baseball burnout" by the time he's 8 or 9.

4. Research the time investment. The time required to participate in some organized sports and activities can be deceptive. Find out all you can about requirements beyond meetings, practices, and games. For example, Lindsey's soccer team practices once a week and plays one game a week for two months each spring. So it's a fairly straightforward schedule that's easily managed. Baseball, on the other hand, is much more involved. Practices and games usually claim Nick two or three times a week, sometimes more. Baseball parents also commit to a once-a-season, day-long turn at the concession stand and a late spring car wash fundraiser. And baseball isn't limited to the regular baseball season. There are preseason and postseason tournaments, all-star teams, fall leagues, etc., that can stretch an expected spring/early summer commitment into a nearly year-round affair.

"Tyler played baseball last year at age 7 from March until November," says Tonya. Making it to the total of more than 70 games during that stretch really slammed a fist into her family's together time, and the whole episode taught them a valuable lesson. "It taught us to guard our downtime to be at home together as a family instead of being at the ballpark every night," she says. "Tyler agreed!"

Other organized activities such as service organizations and clubs often involve regular meetings as well as special events such as parades, service/community projects, banquets, and ceremonies. These "extras" often take chunks of time outside of meeting time to plan, prepare, and attend. Lessons such as dance and gymnastics may call for weekly instruction time on top of additional nights a week as recitals and programs draw near. Often, these programs fall late in the spring, just in time for final tests and major project due dates. The message here is to go into an activity with your eyes wide open. Don't just ask teachers, coaches, and instructors for a rundown of the time commitment; it's their main focus and what you consider to be a large quantity of time may not seem like much to them. A better bet is to ask parents and kids who have been involved in the programs you're considering.

5. Explore the cost. There's no way to prepare parents for the onslaught of "pay for this" and "buy me thats" that raising school-age kids brings. From kids who grow through two shoe sizes each semester to those who need cavities filled and braces installed, sometimes it's almost all we parents—especially those of us in one-income families—can do to keep up with even the basic upkeep of our kids. So when the sign-up sheets start to circulate, we shouldn't feel Scroogish as we closely analyze the merits of each activity to decide how best to spend our budgeted activity and organization dollars.

"We try to choose wisely," says DeAnn, mom of two. "We have to consider whether it is worth it financially. We have a rule, 'If you start it, you have to finish,' so we try to weigh out the pros and cons before we start something new. We don't give them a choice on everything."

To get a clear reading of your investment, always ask up front what's required: Tuition? Deposit? Supply/equipment fees? Beyond that, find out specifically what your dollars will pay for: Art supplies? Hat and jersey? What supplies or equipment will you be expected to buy on your own? Cleats? Find out when and how you'll be expected to pay. Monthly? Yearly? Per lesson? Do you pay for missed lessons? Is there an opportunity to make up missed lessons? Down the road, will there be tournament fees? What about ballpark admission—do parents and siblings pay to see each game? How much will recital costumes run? What about other incidentals that may throw inadvertent blows to your budget: take-out food each Thursday because that's meeting night; concession stand cash, etc. What about the ongoing costs of this new skill or hobby? For example, if your son takes tennis, is there a public tennis court around at which he can fine tune his training? Or will you have to pay a private facility to use its courts each time he wants to play? Finding out specifics now can help you avoid having to head to the bench before the game's over.

6. Consider the nuts and bolts of the schedule: What will the game plan be if you do commit to this activity? For example, when are the lessons or practices held? Do they encroach on church or family commitments? Do they overlap or bump uncomfortably against other commitments? The obligations may fit neatly into your Daytimer: 3:30 den meeting, 4:30 dance, 6:00 ball practice. But in reality those commitments don't fit all that neatly when you consider key details such as kids needing to use the bathroom and have a snack right after school, needing time to change clothes, and needing a decent supper. Allow margins to meet those needs. When the puzzle pieces don't fit, just say no.

7. Get a feel for the environment of the activity or organization. This is a vague one, I know. But try to find out the underlying philosophy of each activity you're considering. If it's a competitive sport, cue in on whether you sense a philosophy of "we want to win at any cost" or the more upbeat attitude of "we're a team and we'll do our best." Do the coaches seem demanding and argumentative or patient and encouraging? Is the service group more concerned with getting their picture in the local paper for the deeds they do or does it involve a group of kids and parents who really stress teamwork and service? Is this activity reinforcing and reminding us of the love God has for our children? Does it exemplify a Christlike life?

Once parents and kids sift through all their options, many choose to become involved in organized sports such as baseball, softball, and soccer. If you're new to the game, you may need a little basic training to help ease you onto the playing field of parenting young athletes.

Sports Sense

The first time I sat through a dismal Little League game holding a flattened popcorn box over my head to keep the rain from dribbling into my eyes, I knew I had a lot to learn about being an effective sports mom.

But Amanda, mother of four (ages 7, 5, 2, and 3 months) whose first foray into sports was a season of T-ball last year, seems to have it all together concerning the bleacher scene: "With a little planning, we as parents can be comfortable in any conditions," she says. She recommends sports families pack the following items in what she calls a "Little League Survival Kit." A duffle or gym bag is perfect, she says, adding that parents should keep it at-the-ready in the closet or car.

Blanket

Sunglasses

Baseball cap (of course!)

Extra hair tie for each girl in the family cheering section

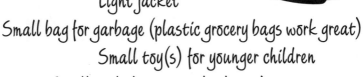

Sunscreen

Lip balm

Tissues

Water bottle

Bag of chips or popcorn

Light jacket

Small bag for garbage (plastic grocery bags work great)

Small toy(s) for younger children

Small pad of paper and a box of crayons

"Obviously some of these items will have to be replenished after each game," she says, "but you get the idea. You can make baseball, or any other sport, an enjoyable experience for your child and the whole family."

There are only a couple more things I might add to Amanda's list: a towel (to sit on, wipe off wet bleachers, dry off wet kids, or swab off muddy cleats) and ... an umbrella!

Keep in mind that not all lessons or activities require joining organizations or even leaving home. Some children prefer to create their own projects and activities and have the determination to work on them. Often checking out "how-to" books or other sports- or activity-specific books from the library can allow your child to develop interest and experiment with activities before you make the commitment leap.

chapter 8

Volunteering: *You Don't Have to Be a Grown-up to Help*

> "Let your light shine before men, that they may see your good deeds and praise your Father in heaven."
> —*Matthew 5:16*

As Christian parents, we all want to teach our kids to take this verse to heart. One great way to do so is through volunteerism in our churches, schools, and communities.

From Scout troop members armed with trash bags and seedlings cleaning up local parks to kindergartners decorating brown paper bags to fill with rice for hungry families, young kids can find many ways to shine God's light in their communities and beyond and share with them the good news of Christ.

"There is a window of opportunity when children ... think it's neat to help people," according to Carol, who plans her church's week-long vacation Bible school each August to revolve around "caring and sharing" projects. That makes nurturing a spirit of volunteerism an easy task, she says. "I don't want to miss that opportunity to instill a lifelong habit of volunteering." Some of the ways she has found for her kindergarten through sixth graders to help others include:

Decorating and filling paper sacks with two pounds of rice from the local rice depot to be distributed to people who need food. The children raised additional funds by turning the event into a "rice-a-

133

thon:" they took pledges from church members for each bag they filled.

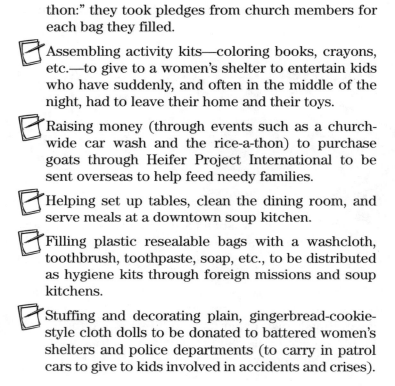

Assembling activity kits—coloring books, crayons, etc.—to give to a women's shelter to entertain kids who have suddenly, and often in the middle of the night, had to leave their home and their toys.

Raising money (through events such as a church-wide car wash and the rice-a-thon) to purchase goats through Heifer Project International to be sent overseas to help feed needy families.

Helping set up tables, clean the dining room, and serve meals at a downtown soup kitchen.

Filling plastic resealable bags with a washcloth, toothbrush, toothpaste, soap, etc., to be distributed as hygiene kits through foreign missions and soup kitchens.

Stuffing and decorating plain, gingerbread-cookie-style cloth dolls to be donated to battered women's shelters and police departments (to carry in patrol cars to give to kids involved in accidents and crises).

Two-Way Street

"Anytime you volunteer, it benefits two ways," says Mavis, an executive director for one Girl Scout Council. "The recipient gets the obvious benefits provided by the service, but the giver gains a boost in self-esteem and self-worth."

Kids who volunteer also "often improve their grades … learn problem-solving processes, form new relationships, and see themselves as members of a community," according to Susan J. Ellis, Anne Weisbord, and Katherine Noyes Campbell in their book, *Children as Volunteers: Preparing for Community Service.*[5]

In addition, Robin, volunteer coordinator for a children's hospital, points out that volunteering is a great way for a young person to hone in on some general career goals. "It's never too early for a child ... to start making some decisions about what he or she would like to do career-wise," she says. "Volunteerism gives them some exposure to lots of behind-the-scenes experiences." In the course of their service, young volunteers might discover a knack, develop a skill, or enhance an existing character trait.

Volunteering also can give youngsters who already know what they would like to be "when they grow up" a chance to lay the groundwork for that career. For example, a young person who would like to become a veterinarian can check into volunteer opportunities at the animal shelter or zoo. A young person who wants to enter the medical profession might explore the world of medicine at the hospital or the Red Cross. A prospective teacher might volunteer by assisting in Sunday school; helping a leader with a younger Scout pack or troop; or tutoring younger students who need help with schoolwork.

66 Being a mom at home can be very rewarding and very stressful. You will never have a clean floor... [because] you clean it and then the floor magnetically attracts juice, milk, water, etc. But being able to attend the school functions, bringing in homemade goodies to the class just because you want to, and seeing your son really proud of you is priceless. There is no job or money that would make up for these moments. 99

—Heather, mother of two

Family Affair

For many families, volunteering is a family affair. In fact, nearly one-fifth of Americans volunteer as a family at least once a week, according to a recent survey.

"We volunteer together," says Marian, coordinator of a volunteer clearinghouse. She says this practice allows parents to promote community service while spending quality time with their kids. "It's a wonderful way to instill in children the philosophy of community participation and service," she says. "As they see you do it and are involved with you as you do it, they'll grow up with it. These are the people who will eventually volunteer later on."

Start Early

"Kids don't have to wait to be big to make a difference in people's lives," Carol says, adding that she discovers this principle time and time again in her work with children.

Pam, another volunteer coordinator, agrees, and believes it's never too early to start nurturing that spirit of service in kids. She recommends that parents "start talking to their kids about helping others at an early age" and remembers explaining to her then-3-year-old why she was going to the downtown soup kitchen to work. After her explanation, her son said, "Mommy, I'm hungry." This, to her, indicated that he was beginning to understand the concept she had been trying to get across.

"Kids need to see that there are people out there who aren't as fortunate as they are," she says. "They need to see that there are actually people who have no home." She also suggests letting young children do chores around the house without giving them an allowance. This, she says, sends a clear message that they shouldn't always expect monetary rewards for their efforts.

"Then, whatever they do, if they really tried, praise them," she says. "Say, 'You should feel really good about that,' rather than, 'You made Mommy happy because you did that' " to foster that sense of inner satisfaction that comes from doing something worthwhile.

Tapping into Opportunities

Kids don't have to go far to make a difference—they can probably even find some opportunities right in their own neighborhoods. In her book, *What Would We Do without You? A Guide to Volunteer Activities for Kids*, Kathy Henderson calls these opportunities "just do its" because they don't require much advanced planning or help to carry out. Take a look at some of her suggestions:

Pick up trash at a neighborhood park.

Sort and save recyclable goods.

Organize a yard sale and donate proceeds to a favorite charity.

Tutor a friend who needs help with a school assignment.

Mow an elderly neighbor's lawn.

Take a first-aid course to get ready to help someone in distress.[6]

Of course, your church is a logical first step in your search for ways to get your kids involved in some sharing and caring projects. Mission classes, vacation Bible schools, and Sunday schools at many churches give kids a chance to join together to help others. A pastor or church secretary can offer the names of organizations and families who need help as well.

Another place where kids can dedicate their time,

energy, and talents to volunteerism is on their own school campus. A school's everyday routine gives kids lots of opportunities to volunteer—whether it's by helping in the library or school office, or by joining a club that places an emphasis on service. And just as Christ modeled a selfless life for us, how better can we model the spirit of volunteerism than by rolling up our sleeves and working at the school ourselves?

Making a Good Match

Finding your child's—and family's—niche in the local squadron of volunteers doesn't always come easily. "Sometimes finding the place to volunteer is more difficult than doing the actual volunteer work," according to Stephanie, director of a volunteer center. She notes that many volunteer-fueled agencies and businesses have minimum age requirements and request that candidates go through sometimes extensive orientation and screening processes. "Volunteering is like being hired; you're just not paid," she says. "Sometimes it takes a while to get on board."

To help with the search, she suggests asking the following questions about each agency or group potential volunteers are interested in approaching:

Can the agency/organization provide you with a position description?

Can it use your skills and time effectively?

Does it offer orientation or materials?

Is it supervised?

What are the requirements?

Has the agency been responsive to you? (Has a representative returned your telephone call or sent you a letter or other information?)

Does it understand your expectations?

Does it offer you a position that fits your interests?

Taking the time to make a careful, educated decision about where you'd like to apply your time and talents pays off, Stephanie says. She urges potential volunteers to "… be selective. Your time is valuable, and a good match will benefit you both."

Scouting: A Tradition of Service

Other service-oriented avenues to explore include traditional organizations such as Girl Scouts and Boy Scouts, which continue to offer kids ample ways to help others.

A field director for the Boy Scouts of America says local troops regularly join forces in such efforts as a "Scouting for Food" campaign held each December to collect staples for his state's food banks and local food pantries, an annual river clean-up, and various other community park clean-up and fix-up days.

"We encourage girls to do service projects for the community and in their neighborhoods," says a Girl Scouts representative. Young Scouts, she says, have cleaned up local schoolyards, stuffed envelopes for a local chamber of commerce, raked leaves for the elderly, and planted flowers and trees in area parks.

"It's very important for girls at a young age to learn to give back to the community that's giving them so much," she says. "We want the girls who go through the Girl Scout program to grow up to be responsible citizens and to contribute to society according to their abilities.

We encourage them to think of other people and be conscious of the needs in the community around them. We live in an environment where there is an awful lot of selfishness. This is teaching them not to be selfish."

Volunteer Opportunities

Check out the following list of organizations that offer volunteer opportunities for kids and/or families.

American Red Cross, American Cancer Society, etc.
These organizations often have volunteer opportunities for almost everyone; age requirements and tasks vary.

Boys and Girls Clubs
These clubs offer kids lots of opportunities to volunteer—from tutoring younger children to community service projects.

Churches
The church is the front line of much of the volunteer work performed in our communities. Check with your pastor, seniors director, or church secretary to find out who and how you can help.

Elderly Activities Programs
Often associations and organizations geared to meet the needs of elderly citizens of your community enjoy putting young enthusiastic volunteers to work in a variety of tasks.

Food Bank Networks/Hunger Relief Organizations
Find out what and where the food bank network/hunger relief organizations are in your community. These organizations provide food to churches, treatment centers, food pantries, and soup kitchens to feed the needy. Volunteers are usually needed to help sort and distribute food.

Hospitals

Sometimes hospitals designate service project days on which groups can come in to do such things as prepare arts and crafts activities for pediatric patients or sing to patients who are able to visit the lobby.

Meals on Wheels

Families can deliver meals to the housebound elderly through this program. Call 1-888-MEAL-HELP.

Museums

Although most of their volunteer slots are more appropriate for the 14-and-over crowd, many museums welcome families with younger children who would like to come in and help with activities and programs.

Parks

They need young people to help with such chores as planting, watering, and keeping the premises litter-free.

Public and Private Schools

Schools need volunteers to serve as tutors, mentors, and classroom aides.

Volunteer Centers/Programs

A great first phone call to find out how and where you can help. Look in your city's yellow pages to find a listing.

Other great volunteer programs include:

The Points of Light Foundation (202-729-8000)

Nickelodeon's The Big Help
PO Box 929, New York, NY 10108
e-mail: bighelp@nickelodeon.com.au
website: www.nickelodeon.com.au/bighelp

Special Olympics (800-700-8585)

Surviving and

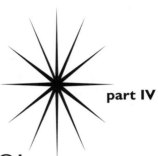

part IV

The Twilight Zone:

Celebrating
the Wacky and Wonderful
World of Mothering

chapter 9

Ecclesiastical Encouragement for Exhausted Moms

> "Let us not become weary in doing good …"—*Galatians 6:9*

From "Watch me write 'pickle' in cursive!" and "Guess how many marshmallows I can fit in my mouth!" to "What do you *do* when you're in heaven?" and "Why does God let those bad guys run around?" kids can bewilder parents with their demands for attention, time, energy, moral guidance, and information.

Although we moms of the physically sufficient school-age set may be expecting to reclaim more of the personal time and independence our infants and toddlers stripped us of, we soon learn that older kids happen to come equipped with a set of just-as-demanding needs.

For example, their sense of spirituality begins to sharpen, prompting "out there" questions and a need for a perceptive mom's or dad's eyes and ears. They are beginning to understand the huge concept of the sacrifice Jesus made for them. Yet their emotional maturity on any given day can dramatically tumble from even-tempered to volatile, or well-adjusted to ultrasensitive, requiring a delicately balanced mixture of tenderness, wisdom, firmness, humor, and/or a handful of homemade chocolate chip cookies. Their social lives begin to blossom, intruding into time we used to call our own and putting us behind the wheel more than we've ever been in our lives.

That sparks the need for our flexibility, diplomacy, and tact. And as if that's not enough, the daily news unleashes a deluge of issues that we must decide if/when/how to discuss with our inquisitive young citizens. Questions about education, sex, extracurricular activities, violence, safety, and budding independence make our worries just a few years ago about nursing, teething, and diaper rash seem like, well, child's play by comparison.

"Developing their understanding of God, [and what's] right and wrong in the world these days" is one of the most formidable challenges Judy, a mom of two, says she faces in her job. DeAnn, homeschooling mom of two, counts finances, and a lack of time to do chores and to be alone as her greatest struggles.

Moms in larger families often say much of their stress comes from trying to meet the individual needs of each of their kids. For example, "My biggest challenges are being able to be involved with all three kids' classes, accomplishing all the homework each day, and keeping up with each child's schedule," says Tula, whose three range in age from 5 to 12. While her goal in being a stay-at-home mom, she says, is to "be available physically as well as spiritually and mentally to better meet the needs of my family," she, like many of us, sometimes finds it difficult to make sure that her own needs in those areas are met as well.

> 66 I like my mom being home ... because she gets to spend time with me and she's here when I need her. 99
>
> —Kathleen, age 9 ½

Andrea also says she finds it tough to divide her time and attention among her three sons. "It's hard sometimes to try to keep everybody balanced," she says.

One morning when I was feeling particularly

stressed over these kinds of mothering problems, I grabbed some quiet time and decided to delve into a chapter of the Bible I had never studied before. I turned to the book of Ecclesiastes, not knowing much about it other than its tranquil tone and the "to everything there is a season" passage. But once I started reading through the

> 66 I like mom being at home ... 'cause there's always someone home when we get home from school. We don't have to look under the doormat for a key. 99
>
> —Caleb, age 9

chapters, I just knew God, in His foresight and grace, had designed them for moms like me who sometimes feel overwhelmed.

Although we might not find that observation in any of our Bible commentaries, I think you'll agree with my assessment after you have a look at some of the following key points I learned as I read.

There is nothing new under the sun.
(Ecclesiastes 1:9)

How comforting to know that moms all the way back to Eve have gone through all the "stuff" we go through each day—big and small. Kids through the ages have had runny noses, the chicken pox, and worse. They've always teethed, been picked on by other children, swallowed things they shouldn't, been rebellious, accidentally broken a neighbor's something-or-other, gotten in trouble at school. Eve could give a heart-rending account of her firsthand experience with sibling rivalry and the loss of a child; Jachobed could describe feeling nearly paralyzed with fear for her son, Moses; and wouldn't it be grand to talk with Mary about both the worries and the wonders of pregnancy—an unexpected one at that! So if you're feeling like you don't know how to handle whatever it is you're going through with your kids, take comfort in the fact that you're not the first! There is indeed nothing new under the sun.

It's not always about "good things."
(Ecclesiastes 2:4–11)

Martha Stewart's trademark comment "It's a good thing" has echoed through thousands of living rooms as many a mom has watched to derive domestic inspiration. Often, as full-time moms, we try to order our world to create a "paradise" within the walls of our homes. We think that making our own jellies, decorating our own gift wrap, growing our own herbs, and throwing the perfect party can be our ticket to Martha's appealing brand of paradise. While these actions in and of themselves are not bad, Ecclesiastes 2 gently points out that nothing *we* can do can give us peace:

> I undertook great projects: I built houses for myself and planted vineyards. I made gardens and parks and planted all kinds of fruit trees in them. I made reservoirs to water groves of flourishing trees ... I also owned more herds and flocks than anyone in Jerusalem before me. I amassed silver and gold for myself, and the treasure of kings and provinces. I acquired men and women singers, and a harem as well—the delights of the heart of man. I became greater

by far than anyone in Jerusalem before me. In all this my wisdom stayed with me. I denied myself nothing my eyes desired; I refused my heart no pleasure. My heart took delight in all my work, and this was the reward for all my labor. Yet when I surveyed all that my hands had done and what I had toiled to achieve, everything was meaningless, a chasing after the wind; nothing was gained under the sun.

Ecclesiastes 2:4–11

It is only through faith in Christ, worked in us by the Holy Spirit, that we can have a portion of peace on earth and receive the lavishly decorated room in the heavenly mansion our Father is lovingly preparing for us.

There is a time for everything.
(Ecclesiastes 3:1–8)

As moms, it's our "time" to do lots of things—in a relatively short amount of time. That calls for us to become experts in time management and masters at the art of prioritizing.

So when you're feeling like you're floundering, and you just don't know how to order your to-do list as you try to juggle the kids, your marriage, the housework, the volunteer work, etc., read Ecclesiastes 3 for a medicinal meditation that will give you a sense of life's rhythm and help you develop some balance. Ecclesiastes 3 tells me that this is a mom's time for:

149

Planting the Word of God in our young ones' hearts, morals in their character, a sense of security in their lives (verse 2).

Building our marriages, our families, our homes on the foundation of His Word (verse 3).

Laughing at the antics of our class clowns, at the hilarity of the crazy situations parenting places us in; laughing to keep from crying (verse 4). "I remember one time my daughter Mindy was cooking, and when she cooks in the kitchen it's everywhere from top to bottom," recalls Sharon. "I could have blown up because within 15 minutes we were all due somewhere, but we started laughing so hard because she had flour on her hands, in her hair, on her eyelashes. I'll never forget Robert had heard us laughing so hard even as he was walking up the deck stairs, and as he slid open the sliding door to our kitchen, he said, 'That was the funnest [sic] thing, to come home and hear the laughter coming out of this kitchen.' I thought to myself, 'If you only knew that 15 minutes earlier, I was about ready to let her have it.' See what a difference that made ... it made it a home of comfort rather than one that could have been so ugly and so growly."

Dancing with a dressed-up son at a mother-son banquet; with other parents in the bleachers as an elated home-run hitter does a celebratory jig after crossing home plate (verse 4).

Embracing our accident-prone gymnast; a tired husband; an 8-year-old soccer player who can't seem to kick in a goal; a 10-year-old whose classmate keeps picking on her (verse 5).

Mending hurt feelings, skinned knees, a misunderstanding-ripped friendship, torn blue jeans—moms are fixers of all things (verse 7).

Being silent tiptoeing out of the bedroom of a sleeping child or keeping our mouths shut when a child is about to do something her own way—which happens to be the sure-fail way. Sometimes we know zipping our lips is the wisest thing to do (verse 7).

Loving—the other word for mothering! (verse 8)

We have a heart full of eternity.
(Ecclesiastes 3:11)

Putting Dreams on Hold

Deciding to stay at home full-time often can derail a woman's plans and dreams. For example, the limited funds of operating a home on just one income may prohibit one mom from pursuing her dream of finishing college. And the time-consuming demands of caring for a growing family may leave no spare minutes for another mom to dabble in the arts and crafts hobby she loves. But putting such dreams on hold doesn't mean having to hit the delete button altogether, Sharon Hoffman points out. As we read in Ecclesiastes 3:1, "There is a time for everything ... under heaven," but that doesn't mean there's time for us to do everything under heaven all at once. Here's Sharon's story:

"There are some things that I put way on the back burner for 21 years, basically, because I knew that I did not have the emotional energy and time because I was raising two daughters in the ministry that the Lord called me to be in," says Sharon. "A lot of the things I put off were desires of my heart that I knew I would not just want to let go in my life. I wrote one book before my second child was born and I began to see that [my writing] was not going to continue while raising two young daughters.

"I found that I was a growly mom, that I was not reasonable. I was crabby and uptight all the time when I was trying to do everything and nothing was ending up being done well.

"I made a conscious choice at that time that you cannot be good at everything. If I was going to be a good writer, then I would have to write; if I was going to be a good mom and wife, then I would have to be a good mom and wife."

So Sharon decided to put down her pen in order to devote her "all" to her daughters. "It was kind of letting go of a dream, but really it was deferring a dream. I always hoped that I would get the opportunity to write again. And I knew if it was of God, I would.

"When I just focused in on the two or three things that, at that stage of my life, I knew were the best things for me to do, then I felt like I gave it my all. I did my very best at those things."

Once her girls left home to forge lives of their own, Sharon says the years she had "given up" for them didn't seem like they had been long at all. In fact, "they seemed like just a blink away." And the dedicated mom's writing aspirations, as it turns out, never boiled dry. In fact, "The very fall that both of our girls went to college ... I began to respond to that yearning to write that I didn't even realize had been so 'there' all along." Once she picked that pen back up, she found two exciting results:

"I was able to be very good at it because that was my major priority of thought, and it also gave me a sense of 'I'm not going through a morbid stage of my life because my girls are grown.' Rather, it opened up doors to a whole exciting phase of my life. I could never be traveling like I do if I had a family at home and I could never close myself in my office and set office hours if I had kids in the home.

"It's been a real wonderful, poignant lesson for me to remember when I have other dreams I'm wanting to fulfill, and am not able to at this time in my life. I remember that what I'm doing right now was on the back burner for years too. So someday I'll get to do those other neat things.

"Moms need to hear that, to let the fire still be on low but to remember that no one else can raise those children."

"I'm having a day." We've all said that from time to time. Sick kids, broken-down cars, a negative checking account balance, dismal weather, appliance malfunctions, doubts about giving up career for home, sibling rivalry that reaches an all-time ferocity. These yucky days are the days when it's easy to lose focus and wish away time by launching into countdowns. "When we get more money …" "When the kids get bigger …" "When ball season is over …"

But "one of our biggest joy stealers is wishing for that next stage of life when we can enjoy the moment," says Sharon Hoffman, author of *Come Home to Comfort*. "We just need to slow down and enjoy the stage of life that we're at right now because it's not going to last forever. At any age that our children are in, we need to live for the moment. The day's going to come when someday you'll wish you had one day of that."

This kind of advice helps snap me back into focus when I'm having "one of those days." It opens my ears to really hear Lindsey when she sings, "God wants me for a sunbeam" to her dolls in her room; to delight, not despair, when she and Nick quarrel over who "gets" to say the dinner prayer; and to notice that Nick's just given Lindsey one of his dollars so she can buy the notebook she wants. Then I realize that I am so grateful to be able to be at home, where I get a minute-by-minute chance to tackle challenges with eternal significance. Solomon said that God has set eternity in our hearts (Ecclesiastes 3:11)—what big cargo for such a humble little boat as me! I have the privilege of not only being able to walk with Christ in my own life, but also becoming the God-designed tugboat that He can use to draw my own precious little ones into His kingdom!

Two are better than one.
(Ecclesiastes 4:9–12)

If you're feeling isolated in your at-home career—if you feel the only places you ever see are your home, the church, and the school—seek out a partner. Naturally, husbands are pretty terrific partners in parenting. But it's still important to find another friend—better yet, more than one—who can help you pick your way through the obstacle course of parenting. My closest friend has kids about the same ages as mine and I wouldn't take a room full of chocolate—no, make that a house full of Cadbury creme-filled eggs—for the encouragement she's given me as I whine to her about my busy calendar, my contrary offspring, my day-long morning sickness, my insecurities—no, my panic attacks—about new projects I've taken on. If you don't have many friends, begin praying today that God will lead you to someone who can fill that role and to whom you, in turn, can minister as well.

You can't take it with you.
(Ecclesiastes 5:15)

I used this quote in my first book, *Celebrate Home*, and it's so good that I can't resist using it again here: "… I know that I can't get to heaven pulling my little red wagon full of all my things," said Diana Ferrell, "But maybe, with the grace of God, I can get there with my children." If you are having doubts as to whether you should remain at home because it seems just too

> 66 I like my mom being at home …
> because if she wasn't home,
> we wouldn't see her that much. 99
> —Tyler, age 9

tough to make ends meet on one income, remember that God has much to say about the insignificance of wealth and at each turn He promises to provide for our every need. Rather than asking, "Can we afford to keep sacrificing one income in order for me to stay at home?" ask yourself, "How can we afford for me *not* to make our family and kids a priority?" It's not easy to pinch pennies day in and day out, especially in this society that tells us to spend, spend, spend. But it does get easier with practice and perseverance! "Better one handful with tranquility than two handfuls with toil and chasing after the wind" (Ecclesiastes 4:6).

These are the days!
(Ecclesiastes 9:7)

Mothering is a stressful job. There's just no way around it. It's physically demanding, and it takes us on a roller coaster of emotions. The kicker is that while we're doing it we're expected to carry out an endless number of additional roles: wife, daughter, friend, church member, soccer coach, parent-teacher volunteer, informed citizen, cautious consumer ... but when you're feeling overwhelmed, just take a few minutes and meditate on this verse. It's a love letter from God: "Go, eat your food with gladness, and drink your wine with a joyful heart, for it is *now* that God favors what you do" (Ecclesiastes 9:7, emphasis added).

chapter 10

Trading Chaos for Comfort

"For God is not a God of disorder but of peace."—*I Corinthians 14:33*

It's a life of chaos instead of comfort some days," says Sharon Hoffman, mother of two grown daughters who remembers all too well the hectic pace of being a full-time mom to two busy daughters. "There are days when we're frazzled, and we're fussy, and we're about to faint … but they don't last forever."

How, as moms, can we convert some of that chaos to comfort?

Organizing our world—our surroundings as well as our calendar—can help us and our homes operate as efficiently as possible. Books and magazine articles abound on clutter control, household organization, and time management. Check out some of those books and use only the hints that will help *you*. Don't take on "organization" chores that will defeat your purpose because they require preparations too elaborate or chunks of time too long to implement! Maybe buying a couple of pads of sticky notes or a dry erase board to post reminders will help you better keep your household running on track. Streamlining some of your cleaning and/or laundry routines might free up some time and restore some order. A top-to-bottom closet and drawer cleaning day might be just the trick. Or maybe getting into the habit of making lunches the night before is all it takes to calm the craziness of the morning rush. Following are some trouble spots moms say cause the most turmoil at home, and some ways to smooth them out.

Sunday Mornings

Sunday morning starts on Saturday night for moms who want to avoid pre-church pandemonium. One mom in a long-ago MOPS discussion group said she dressed her kids for Sunday school on Saturday night and that way they were practically ready to go—although a little wrinkled—when they woke up. You may not want to take your advance preparations to that extreme but you can lay out clothes for little ones and help older ones select what they want to wear the next day. That way you'll avoid last-minute ironing or searching sessions and, consequently, you'll prevent that mad dash back home to make sure you turned the iron off after you've already turned in to the church parking lot. Lay out Bibles, offering envelopes, quarterlies, and any other materials you need and make sure the kids (and you) get to bed at a decent hour. Pack as much of the diaper bag as you can the night before too. On Sunday morning, you don't necessarily need to get everyone up at the same time; early risers can get in and out of the bathrooms before the late ones. Get everyone up in plenty of time to allow for some lolling around—you don't want this special day to feel like a typical school or work day. But don't try to pay bills, mow the grass, or do that extra load of laundry. Somehow Sunday mornings deceive us into thinking we have more time than we actually do. Save the hearty bacon, eggs, toast, and pancake breakfast for Saturday mornings; set serve-it-yourself bagels or cornflakes on the counter on Sundays. Concentrate on your task at hand: just getting everyone ready and out the door on time, with a minimum of bickering and barking.

Before Ball Games

Make a habit of keeping game gear together. Designate one hook or shelf for gloves, caps, helmets, rackets, etc. When your sport comes in from each game, her first stop should be to park her stuff there. The next stop should be to peel off the uniform, which, in an ideal world you'll immediately inspect for grass and/or mud stains that should be pre-treated with a squirt of stain remover now, before being tossed into the dirty clothes hamper. After the uniform's been washed, roll all of its parts up together and put them in the same corner of the same drawer each time. Have a special on-the-way-out-the-door caddy stocked with change and dollars (concession money, game admission) to draw from as you and the team head out the door. This is also where you can leave signed permission slips, picture order forms, and anything else that has to get to the game with your child.

Before Birthday Parties

A good birthday party routine starts when you get the invitation. When you dig it out of the backpack or mailbox, check your calendar right away. If there's no conflict, mark it in ink, noting all the pertinent info: time, location, directions, and parents' names and phone number in case you lose the invitation.

If an RSVP is required, respond while it's fresh on your mind. Even if an RSVP isn't required, any mom who's planning a party appreciates a call anyway. That gives her a chance to form a better head count and you a chance to let her know how tickled your child is to have been invited. This also gives you a way to find out more helpful info: Will you drop off or stay with the child? What should your child wear? After you've made the call, hang the invite on the fridge or bulletin board as a reminder. Add "birthday gift" to your shopping list. Some moms keep a stash of age-and-gender-appropriate gifts year-round to avoid last-minute shopping trips. I'm usually a stop-by-the-store-on-the-way kind of mom. I keep a pair of scissors, a roll of tape, and a pen in the glove box of the van at all times. That way, after we've dashed in to buy the gift, card, and gift sack or paper, the kids can take over wrapping the present and signing the card en route.

Before heading to the party, stick the invitation in your purse or on your dashboard so you'll have the directions, a reminder of the parents' names if you don't know them very well, and a phone number in case you run into a snag. (We ran into one not too long ago. Heading to a horseback riding party about 30 minutes out of town, Lindsey and I drove through a deluge of rain. We were sure the party would have to be cancelled. I had the number with me and called the horse farm to check in. As it turned out, it wasn't raining there. About 15 minutes later, we drove out of the rain. If I hadn't been able to call, I probably would have turned around for home, I had been so sure the party was rained out.)

After School

The skinned knee on the playground, the test results, the ins and outs of the teacher's new reading incentive program ... many moms catch meaty stream-of-consciousness newsflashes during this golden drive time after school. Everyone's happy to be out of school and to see their favorite grown-up woman in the world, and they all want to tell her about their day—all at once. This time is the jackpot for info-hungry moms who usually manage to jot all the tidbits onto a mental notepad to retrieve for later sorting, filing, and saving. But once home, the giving seems to stop and the requests, quarrels, and demands turn into a challenge that seems to be more than one human can handle. "I'm starving!" "I don't want to watch that! He always gets to pick." "I need a poster board to do my project for tomorrow." "I'm bleeding!" Many of us consider herding our flock back to the front door past the trail of jackets, shoes, socks, backpacks, lunchboxes, and umbrellas they shed as they filed in, into the van, and back to school. But we usually decide not to do this, because we know that they're just decompressing after a long day. We patiently begin to tackle one request at a time—using all eight arms God gave us—and we slowly calm the after-school storm into a contented lull. Here are some tips to help you survive the after-school buzz.

Pack a snack. When kids say they're starving or thirsty after school, they usually aren't exaggerating. The structure of school days usually calls for staggered lunchtimes that mean some kids have to eat as early as 10:45 or 11:00 A.M. By the time they get in the car, they understandably have a severe case of the growlies. Consider packing a little snack in the car so they can start munching when you pick them up. That way, when you walk in the door at home, their hunger and thirst won't be so urgent.

Start a pile. If you don't have an on-the-way-in spot to stash jackets and backpacks, at least teach your kids to control the clutter by tossing them in one designated corner until they've had a chance to finish their snack and get some of their wiggles out. Then they can put things where they belong. In the meantime, you won't be tripping over the debris of the day and you won't have to start nagging right away.

Start a comfortable routine. If vegging in front of the TV for a few minutes is what your kids like to do when they get home, let them. Better yet, curl up beside them and take a break yourself. Don't bombard them with questions about homework, suggestions about what they could be doing now, or reminders about chores. Give them a few minutes to decompress. On the other hand, if they come in and start nervously rattling around like monkeys in a cage, have some activity suggestions ready (see Chapter 5 for ideas). After a day spent on a structured schedule, they may feel uncomfortable or out of control given too much latitude. A little direction might be just what they need to help them focus their energy.

Before Dinner

When I'm stressing about getting dinner ready and the kids are being unruly, I put on my captain's hat and start barking out orders and doling out chores. "Set the table." "Do your homework." "Unload the dishwasher." That way, the kids will either stay out from underfoot to avoid being assigned a duty or they'll be gainfully occupied helping me get jobs done. Let the machine or the kids answer the phone while you're preparing dinner. Chances are, at this time of day, it's a telemarketer anyway because most of your friends are moms right in the middle of their dinner preparation too. If dinner's running a bit late and the kids are begging for food, resist the motherly urge to say "but it will ruin your supper" and instead offer some carefully chosen "appetizers" that you can consider as a down payment on their meal. Let them go ahead and eat their salad, restaurant style, or nibble on a few slices of fruit, or munch some crackers spread with butter. Getting something in their tummies will calm the savage beasts, at least until you can finish fixing the main course.

Bedtime

To avoid bedtime bedlam, set a turn-in time for school nights and church nights—and stick with it. We've been moms long enough now to know how important getting enough sleep is to our kids' health and frame of mind. Experts say most elementary school kids need 9–10 hours of sleep a night. Some need more, especially during seasons with extra and exciting activities such as the Christmas holidays; springtime when the weather's nice and they're more physically active; and the end of the school year when class work is likely to be intense.

Offer a light snack before toothbrushing and form—and stay with—a comforting bedtime rhythm. It may include an "in-the-bed-time" that's 30 minutes earlier then the "lights out time" to allow for a story; a prayer or devotional; a backscratch; personal reading time; journal writing time; some one-on-one pillowtalk; and goodnight kisses. Start homework early enough so that the kids won't have to close the book and hop into bed without any downtime. Do all you can up front to prevent having to fill those requests kids often use to keep you yo-yoing back to their room five times after lights out. For example, don't leave the room for the last time until you've made sure they've used the bathroom, covered all of the day's scrapes and wounds with bandages, turned on the bedtime music and/or night light, left a cup of water by their bed, rolled up an extra blanket at the foot of the bed, adjusted the ceiling fan, retrieved the favorite doll or snuggly, and taken care of any other needs—you know what they are—that crop up.

66 My mother was always at home for us. She was always there to listen when we got home from school. As a pre-teen, that was pretty important, and in hindsight, it kept me out of a lot of trouble. 99

—Harriett, mother of one

Too Pooped to Parent?
Take Some Personal Time

Does this scenario describe times at your house?

"... So many people were coming and going that they did not even have a chance to eat." That's from a Scripture passage in Mark describing the apostles as they were hustling and bustling around Jesus. Seeing how frazzled they had become, He quickly suggested that they "take five:" "Come with Me by yourselves to a quiet place and get some rest," He urged (Mark 6:31). So the group piled into a nearby boat and beat a hasty retreat "to a solitary place."

If that's a self-care tactic endorsed by the Savior of the world, shouldn't we moms give it a try?

Do you have a solitary place? You may not be able to hop on a boat and head for a remote tropical island, but maybe you can grab certain times to take a break for rest and restoration. High on my list of restful breaks are: the rare weekend getaway with my husband; a Sunday afternoon spent at my mom and dad's house; and the occasional nights when I'm so exhausted that I decide to climb into bed before the rest of my family. (I'll tell everybody goodnight, announce that I'm "off duty," shut my door, and read until I fall asleep.)

"One thing that I like to remember is when I'm really feeling that chaos closing in, it's a signal that I need to take some time for me," says Sharon. "Every day in our lives we need to take time for our own hearts."

For Sharon, and for many moms, taking care of herself starts with a daily quiet time first thing each morning. "Of course, our source of comfort is only the Comforter, and that's the Lord Jesus. It all starts in our hearts and then we can put it in our homes," she says.

"Some people say, 'I'm not a morning person,' but I

guarantee if you go through one month of having some quiet time with the Lord and with the Scriptures, even if it's five minutes, to set the tone for the day, or to hide God's Word in your heart, then when the weariness and the hectic schedules set in and invade our hearts throughout the day, we can remember those moments that we spent with Him earlier. I love to encourage women to do that. It makes a big difference."

Here are some other destinations moms sail off to when they need to rest and revive:

"With all three in school, I try to set aside one morning a week for a bath, a book, or whatever I would like to do," says Tula. *"I also take an in-depth Bible study course at church one evening a week."*

"The best thing I do is attend a women's Bible study at our church," says DeAnn, mom of two. *"I also take time to read. I'll stay up occasionally after everyone else is in bed and read, or write in my journal, or every once in a while watch TV. Other times, I'll take an afternoon nap or go to bed early."*

"A walk in the morning and quiet time with the Lord" is her best daily getaway, says Tonya.

"I schedule [mom time]—into my calendar—Bible study classes, that is!" says Gina. *"The personal study time is more 'catch-as-catch-can' or burning the midnight oil."* She also loves to *"have lunch with friends, even if it is burgers in McDonald's playland so the kids can run around while we visit!"* Dinner and/or a movie with her husband also rates high on her mothercare chart, she says.

"Take time to have a glass of iced tea or pour a cup of coffee and light a candle and slow your mind down for a moment," says Sharon. *"That makes the home a refuge rather than a chaotic, hectic place before everybody starts running in for dinner."*

Putting Comfort into Our Homes

Sharon Hoffman, author of *Come Home to Comfort*, knows all kinds of ways to add peace and tranquility to the home. "Put a comfort of hugging your family into the home," she says, by "plugging in a little potpourri pot ... that makes a welcoming home when you walk in. Make it a place that it's fun to come home to. I encourage women to grab up that little bundle of flowers at the grocery store. Treat yourself once in a while to those fresh flowers. It's something that soothes your spirit. I used to feel like 'that's a luxury,' and it is, but it perks up everybody's spirit.

"Little tips like that don't cost much or take a lot of time but can really make us feel special. It shows our families, 'Hey, you're important enough for me to do this for. I don't just do it for company or for holidays.' "

Ultimately, we can't go from disorder to peace, from chaos to comfort, through our own deeds—as efficient, organized, and thoughtful as we may try to be. Comfort isn't a freedom from troubles and hassles but a gift which produces "patient endurance" in the midst of troubles and hassles (2 Corinthians 1:6).

**"For just as the sufferings of Christ
flow over into our lives, so also through
Christ our comfort overflows."
(2 Corinthians 1:5)**

Afterword

My Editor

Confidently crossing through a seven-word phrase with my red felt-tip pen and replacing it with two words, I turned, ... *and come to a point of understanding* into the more concise, ... *and understand.*

Then I crossed out the piece's final three sentences, which belabored the point and made for a slow ending. Next I made a last-minute switch in the order of the chapters. Mission accomplished, I tossed the pen on my desk and leaned back in my chair to reread the edited version of the hardcopy. I had trimmed a flabby, 40,000-word manuscript down to a lean and punchy 36,000 words.

Too bad I can't do that to my own life, I thought, as I considered how the activities that make up my days only rarely fit neatly within the margins. More often, they spill into the borders or are even hastily inserted as last-minute revisions across the pages of my life.

My grammatical style is all wrong too. When I should be writing my evenings by using passive verbs—listening to music with my daughter, being read to by my son, or being fascinated by my husband's latest improvement to his electric train set—I am too often firing an artillery of active verbs, barking out orders about bathtime, and frantically digging through the pockets of dirty laundry in search of two quarters because tomorrow is popcorn day at school and I have no change to send.

Yet when I ought to be putting active verbs to work by swimming with my daughter, playing catch with my son, or walking around the neighborhood with my husband, I'm likely to be passively basking in the sun, sitting on the sidelines, or climbing into bed because I'm just too pooped.

But as they say, every writer needs an editor. Even if I were able to eliminate all my redundant actions, inject succinct meaning into my every effort, and get my word count just right, my story would still be lacking because I'm not perfect.

But I am thankful that I know Someone who is. He is present perfect, past perfect, and future perfect. He's the first and last letters of the alphabet. He's the only one who knows the end of my book from the beginning; in fact, He's the author and finisher of my salvation.

So I'll just keep cranking out the best hard copy I can, and humbly turn each page over to Christ. The red marks He made 2,000 years ago are turning my copy into a flawlessly clean manuscript.

Family Night

What is it?

Whether you're celebrating a family member's Baptism birthday or learning about setting goals, family night is a wonderful way to create memories, build family unity, and just plain have fun.

What's in it?

A well-thought-out family night will include an activity, a teaching time, a game, a special meal, and prayer. "Variety is another thing that is really important," Bonnie says. "And they love to be surprised. One of our favorite things would be a surprise marshmallow fight! Whatever you can do that's a little unpredictable."

How much time should it take?

An hour and a half to two hours (except when you plan longer outings such as picking apples or chopping down your Christmas tree) is usually plenty of time. Bonnie suggests parents limit the teaching time to five minutes for young children and 10–15 minutes for older kids.

How often should we plan it?

Start small, Bonnie says. "I think you could start with once or twice a month and get your feet wet. I don't think there were very many months that we did four. We try to encourage people not to get under the pile, thinking this is another thing on their 'to-do' list every week. Start small, plan one that's really fun, and see what the kids like. If they like it, they'll ask, 'When are we going to do it again?' "

Resources

Choosing Home

The Newsletter for At-Home/Work-at-Home Moms

P.O. Box 3191
Syracuse, NY 13220-3191
Phone/fax: 1-888-698-0857
choosinghome@scctel.com
http://www.angelfire.com/biz/ChoosingHome

Janice M. Boyles, publisher of *Choosing Home*, compiles a variety of information about subjects ranging from mothering, work-at-home career choices, and budgeting, to book reviews, how-tos, and much more in this monthly publication.

Moms in Touch International

P.O. Box 1120
Poway, CA 92074-1120
800-949-MOMS

www.europa.com/~philhow/moms_in_touch.html

Moms in Touch International challenges moms to be involved in their children's lives through prayer by meeting an hour each week to pray for their children and their schools. Contact MITI to see if there are other moms praying in your area or to start an MITI prayer group.

The Family Corner

www.thefamilycorner.com

This resource offers information and advice about parenting, family, home and garden, being a mom, self-esteem, fitness, dieting, and more. Operated by Amanda Formaro.

Hearts at Home

900 W. College Ave.
Normal, IL 61761
309-888-6667
www.hearts-at-home.org
e-mail: hearts@dave-world.net

Imagine being at a conference with 5,000 other stay-at-home moms. If you're the only stay-at-home mom on your block, like I am, it's an experience you won't soon forget. Hearts at Home regional conferences feature noted speakers and workshop presenters who address all kinds of topics of interest to moms—from parenting issues to marriage to personal enrichment. This non-denominational, Christ-centered, professional organization is designed for mothers at home or those who want to be. The group desires to exalt God while educating and encouraging women in their personal and family lives. Services and resources in addition to the regional conferences include publications (a devotional and a monthly magazine), audio and video-tapes, and products for mothers at home.

National Association of At-Home Mothers

At-Home Mothers' Resource Center

406 E. Buchanan Ave.
Fairfield, IA 52556
www.athomemothers.com

The National Association of At-Home Mothers was founded as a professional organization unaffiliated with any religious or political group, offering practical information, inspiration, services, support, and encouragement for mothers at home and those who would like to be.

MOPS International

1311 S. Clarkson St.
Denver, CO 80210
303-733-5353
http://www.mops.org

This Christian organization is designed to nurture mothers of preschoolers. With chapters in more than 950 churches in the United States, MOPS also has a Mission MOPS program established in eight foreign countries. To find out if there is a MOPS chapter near you, contact MOPS International, Inc., or check out their website.

WAHM—Work at Home Moms

http://www.wahm.com

WAHM is an online magazine for moms who work at home. "WAHM is for moms who are trying to balance a family and home business, and also for the working moms who are thinking about leaving the traditional workplace," says founder Cheryl Demas, who left her engineering career and became an at-home mom when her 7-year-old daughter was diagnosed with diabetes just three days before her little sister was born. ("That was quite a week," she says.)

"WAHM is dedicated to promoting work-at-home moms' businesses, providing information about legitimate work-at-home opportunities, and providing tips, advice, and entertainment to work-at-home moms everywhere," says Cheryl.

WAHM sponsors two mailing lists—one for all work-at-home moms and another, WebMoms, for moms in the web design business. Cheryl says she may add more job-specific lists if there is sufficient interest, and she has already launched a print version of the newsletter. For more information, check out their website or write Maricle Software, Box 366, Folsom, CA 95763.

Welcome Home

Mothers at Home

> 8310A Courthouse Road
> Vienna, VA 22182
> 703-827-5903
> www.mah.org/wh_periodical.html

Written, edited, and illustrated by and for mothers, *Welcome Home* is an award-winning monthly journal offering stories about mothers' struggles and successes, informative articles about family life and public policy issues, mother-to-mother problem solving, humor, poetry, and more.

Endnotes

1 For more information about planning a family night for your family, including suggested plans for family nights, see *Making Family Memories: A Family Night Planner*, by Rich and Bonnie Skinner, published by FamilyLife, a division of Campus Crusade for Christ, 1998. (1-800-FL-TODAY; http://www.familylife-ccc.org)

2 Susan Alexander Yates, "How to Choose the Best School for Your Child," *Today's Christian Woman*, May/June 1996.

3 Joan Bergstrom, *School's Out, Now What?* (Berkeley, California: Ten Speed Press, 1984) page 8.

4 Ibid., page 25.

5 Susan J. Ellis (editor), Katherine Noyes Campbell (editor), Trina Tracy, and Anne Weisbord. *Children as Volunteers: Preparing for Community Service.* (Philadelphia, Pennsylvania: Energize Books, 1991).

6 Kathy Henderson, *What Would We Do without You? A Guide to Volunteer Activities for Kids* (White Hall, Virginia: Betterway Publications, 1990).